THE

ART OF

Winning

Corporate

Grants

THE
ART OF
Winning
Corporate
Grants

BY HOWARD HILLMAN

Coauthor: Marjorie Chamberlain

THE VANGUARD PRESS, INC.   NEW YORK

*This book is dedicated to
the American capitalistic system
that creates the profits
that pay for the grants*

CONTENTS

PREFACE

Two billion dollars of corporate money will flow this year into the hands of worthy causes such as yours. Add on items such as gifts deducted on the corporate tax return as ordinary business expenses rather than charitable donations, and corporate largess reaches $4 billion annually. Corporations are indeed a major funding source.

Please do not draw erroneous conclusions from these figures. Corporate philanthropists are not signing checks with a pen in each hand, and you are not the only deserving prospective recipient. Competing for the same funds are hundreds of thousands of nonprofit agencies, including hospitals, federated campaigns such as the United Way, libraries, environmental protection groups, drug rehabilitation services, schools, and cultural centers. Individuals also receive a share of the corporate-philanthropy pie, in the form of scholarships and research grants.

By learning the art of winning corporate grants, you can gain an invaluable edge over your competition, because most fund-seekers have limited knowledge of the corporate funding process and how it differs from those of other philanthropic sources. Although there is some overlap in the methodology of corporate philanthropy versus foundation and governmental-agency giving, there are critical differences. Our book will help you understand those distinctions.

Much research went into this book. Besides borrowing from our past expertise, we read millions of published words on corporate philanthropy and social responsibility. We also sought the facts firsthand by interviewing corporate personnel on all relevant levels, from chairpersons of the board down to members of employee-contributions committees. Finally, insiders' tips and insights were graciously contributed to us by scores of successful corporate grant-seekers.

Our next task was just as arduous as the research phase. We

distilled the voluminous data into a quick-to-grasp, step-by-step format designed for busy, intelligent grant-seekers, be they experienced pros or laypersons.

We cannot, of course, guarantee your success, but we do know that if you read this book, your chances of winning corporate gifts will increase markedly. Just as important, our book will save you the cost of going down the wrong roads.

INTRODUCTION

No one has yet fashioned the master key to the corporate treasury, not only because each corporate giving-program is distinct, but also because the goals of each grant-seeker are singular.

Although we cannot offer you the magical master key, we can give you a complete set of tried and proven keys that, when used in conjunction with a fundable project, will help you unlock the corporate treasury.

KEY 1   Know Why Corporations Give
KEY 2   Know To Whom Corporations Give
KEY 3   Know What Corporations Give
KEY 4   Know How Corporations Give
KEY 5   Know Thyself
KEY 6   Research/Research/Research
KEY 7   Develop Creative Tie-Ins
KEY 8   Meet With The Corporation
KEY 9   Write The Winning Proposal
KEY 10   Follow Through

These ten keys are discussed individually in the sections that follow.

PART ONE

Ten Keys to the Corporate Treasury

Know Why Corporations Give

Contrary to what some corporate PR departments would have you believe, corporations seldom if ever give for purely altruistic reasons. For a grant-seeker to hold such a Pollyanna notion is a counterproductive self-delusion of the first rank. When a grant-seeker misconceives the true motives for corporate giving, the appeal to the corporation misses the mark and is unpersuasive. Moreover, by entertaining fanciful ideas of what a corporation wants, the grant-seeker will be off-target when the time comes to develop natural match-ups between his or her needs and the corporation's needs.

The first and foremost law of corporate giving is that virtually all donations are made in the self-interest of the corporation and/or its decision-makers.

To approach a corporation on the assumption that it will fund you simply because you have a good cause is naive. That approach may work with foundations and government agencies (if your project is the best of those that meet the donor's goals), but with corporations you will almost certainly need to offer a benefit to the firm's short- or long-term profit-making structure, or to the executives' well-being. More about those concepts later.

In a widely published and quoted survey, several hundred corporate chairpersons and presidents were asked to give the reasons for corporate philanthropy: "good corporate citizenship" (a facet of social responsibility) was the chief rationale cited. We do not believe that the results of that poll are sufficiently realistic, because there is a built-in bias: The executives naturally wanted to present their companies to the public in a favorable light, so the self-assessments tended to be in a self-congratulatory vein. Furthermore, the list of ten answers that the surveyed executives were asked to check were too vague, brief, and limited in scope to give a grant-seeker much insight into the corporate decision-making processes. For those reasons, we consider the following set of motives to be more detailed, comprehensive, and realistic.

Motive: To Get a Tax Write-off

A tax-write-off advantage does exist for corporations, but not to the degree that some grant-seekers believe.

Except in a few special situations, it costs money for a corporation to make a donation. The amount a corporation saves in taxes generally covers only a part of the cost of the gift. To illustrate, let us assume that a corporation's tax rate is approximately 50 percent (a typical figure) and that it gives a $10,000 check to a charity. On its income tax return, the corporation will be able to deduct $10,000 from its pretax earnings and thus will save approximately $5,000 in taxes. The bottom line, however, is that the gift costs the corporation $5,000, the difference between the amounts of the gift and of the tax-savings. If tax write-offs for donations were directly profitable, you can be sure that more corporations would be giving to charity the full 5 percent of their pretax earnings allowed by law. Currently, the average percentage figure hovers around 1 percent.

What the tax write-off does, is lower the philanthropic cost to the corporation, since the government shares approximately half the cost of the gift, creating sort of a matching-gift instrument. In effect, the corporation is doubling the impact of each after-tax dollar it gives. Two-for-one is not a bad bargain.

So if the tax-write-off advantage is not consequential enough to entice more than a few corporations to deduct the 5 percent maximum legal limit, it does offer some inducement. As proof, consider what would happen if the tax write-off were annulled. Most corporate philanthropic budgets would be quickly and decisively pared.

Motive: To Build a Positive Public Image

Philanthropy is one of the few effective tools that a corporation can use to project a saintly image in the eyes of the general public. If a corporation lowers prices or improves its product, the customer will probably be happy but will not necessarily think of the corporation in endearing terms. Consider your different reactions as John Q. Public if you heard that Chevrolet was lowering the price of 10,000 of its cars by $100 each, as opposed to being informed that Chevrolet was donating the equivalent amount ($1 million) to the Boy Scouts of America.

Motive: To Influence Opinion-makers

One percent of the United States' population—approximately 2.5 million people—exercise a lot of clout in determining how the rest of the country thinks on the environment, price increases, and other major complex issues. Large corporations are well aware of this phenomenon.

What is an ideal vehicle for reaching these typically more affluent, better educated opinion makers? The Public Broadcasting System. While the size of the PBS audience is small compared to a prime-time network sit-com audience, PBS viewers comprise most of America's one-percenters.

People uninitiated in the public relations discipline may wonder what good accrues to the corporation if all it gets for its sizable gift is a brief "Funding was made possible by the XYZ Corporation" credit. The answer is simple. The XYZ Oil Company, to use an example, knows that when it raises gas prices or has an accidental oil spill, many of the one-percenters will not be as harsh on the company because "those are the good guys who sponsor the Shakespeare plays on TV." The underlying strategy of this type of a PR program is not necessarily to get the one-percenters to look favorably upon the company; a firm will get its money's worth if it can just neutralize the one-percenters, that is, keep them from thinking badly of it.

Motive: To Cultivate Stockholder Goodwill

Top executives are chosen by the board of directors, who in turn are elected by the stockholders, a group that must be reckoned with when designing and implementing a philanthropic program. This is especially true if stock ownership is concentrated in a few hands. For a more detailed discussion on the stockholder's role in charitable contributions, see "The Great Debate: Should Corporations Give?" (page 11).

Motive: To Build Business Community Relations

Few corporations operate in a vacuum within their community, because business destinies can be altered by influential executives of other community-based organizations.

As a case in point, let us assume that a corporation needs a loan and the bank's pros and cons for approving it are fifty–fifty. Obviously, the bank's decision-making scale may well be tipped in the corporation's favor if the banker thinks well of that firm because of its current support of local charities.

Motive: To Please Other Special Publics

Corporations have many other special publics to please besides the ones mentioned above. The list also includes

> Activist groups
> Competitors
> Consumers
> Governmental agencies
> Journalists

                       Legislators
                       Politicians
                       Religious leaders
                       Trade organizations
                       Trade unions

Motive: To Return a Favor

Six months ago the president of the Alpha Corporation chaired a fund-raising drive for Charity X and obtained a $5,000 gift from the president of the Beta Corporation, who now happens to be heading a campaign for Charity Y. It probably will not take much effort to get the Alpha Corporation to write out a $5,000 check to Charity Y. The "I supported yours, now you support mine" deal is more prevalent than most people suspect. An IOU is an IOU.

Motive: To Keep Up with the Jones Corporation

Many a top executive has mused, "If our competition and the company across the road are donating a certain percentage of their pretax income to charity, shouldn't we, too?"

Motive: To Perpetuate the Past

Some "ditto-mentality" corporate executives rubber-stamp the philanthropic programs that they inherited from their predecessors because "Pat must have had a reason for it." Little thought is given to whether the philanthropic budget should be axed, trimmed, preserved, or increased.

Motive: To Support Employee Services

Corporations readily recognize the value of contributions to community organizations that provide needed services to the firm's employees. Fitting that definition would be, for instance, a tuberculosis detection project that provided free X-ray checkups.

Motive: To Foster Employee Training

Trained personnel are essential to a corporation's economic livelihood. That is why many corporations assign a sizable share of their corporate philanthropy budget to colleges and universities as well as to technical schools. Far-sighted firms look upon this funding as an investment rather than as a charitable act.

Motive: To Increase Productivity

A byproduct of philanthropic spending can be increased employee productivity and job satisfaction. If many of a corporation's skilled laborers live in a ghetto and the company makes a substantial grant to a ghetto cause, most industrial relations experts would agree that employees' pride in their company will improve.

Motive: To Entice Prospective Employees and Transferees

A large corporation must hire a steady supply of bright, young, college graduates to train for eventual management duties. Such prospective employees are often unexcited about taking a job in a community lacking sufficient cultural activities and intellectual stimulation, as a recent survey of Wharton School of Finance graduate students confirmed.

Corporations have another problem: convincing their existing executives to transfer to communities lacking an adequate ambiance and level of culture.

Yet another problem: Even if the recruit or executive is willing, the spouse may not be.

Corporations, therefore, will donate money to cultural organizations in the hope of upgrading the community's cultural environment.

A secondary recruitment-related benefit for giving to local cultural institutions is image-building. When the recruiter describes the corporation's financial backing of cultural endeavors, the firm will seem less impersonal, more people-oriented in the minds of most prospective management-trainees and executive-level employees.

Motive: To Insure against Future Losses

At times the repercussions of not giving outweigh the cost of giving. Situations exist in which haggling with government officials in and out of court or rebuilding a factory gutted during a riot will cut more deeply into corporate profits than a gift. "Philanthropic insurance" is what one executive called it.

Motive: To Associate with Quality

Texaco has been loyally sponsoring Metropolitan Opera broadcasts for nearly fifty years because it knows that many listeners link the corporation's reputation with that of the illustrious cultural ensemble. A glance at the sponsor lists of PBS and cultural centers will demonstrate how many corporations enjoy basking in the light of another's respectability. It works.

Motive: To Satisfy the Executive's Personal Desires

The above-mentioned motives concern indirect gains for the corporation. Benefits to the decision-making executive are a powerful motive, too.

Some executives look upon their control of the corporate philanthropic budget as a fun toy and with the perquisite of being able to select recipients, an opportunity to play god. Others receive unselfish satisfaction that they are able to give to charity (albeit with the corporation's money).

Executives can also use the philanthropic program as a tool for career advancement. With the power that goes along with the philanthropic dollar comes an opportunity to make valuable business contacts and to receive personal publicity. Empire building is also an incentive. If executives can coax a greater philanthropic budget out of their board of directors, they enhance their positions within the corporate framework.

Charity balls, cultural affairs, and similar undertakings are often funded because the decision-making executive and spouse enjoy attending those occasions, be they a glittering New Year's Eve ballroom dance or a performance of Beethoven's Ninth Symphony. As the promotors of events such as celebrity tennis tournaments know, many executives relish rubbing elbows with the famous.

Motive: To Give from the Heart, But Only If . . .

As we have previously stated, pure altriusm as a motive is a rare flower in the jungle of corporate philanthropy. Few grant-seekers have ever sniffed its scent. Businesses give, we must emphasize, principally because giving is good business.

We do not mean to suggest that altruism is a nonexistent force. After all, most corporate executives are not ogres or philistines; like the rest of us, they are sensitive to the plight of the needy and are moved by the works of artists. However, corporations do not give with the same degree of unselfishness as would a private person who follows Matthew's Biblical advice:

> When you give alms, do not let your left hand know what your right hand is doing so that your alms may be a secret.

The corporate altruistic bud blooms when and only when it is known that the gift will benefit and not backfire on the corporations and/or its executives. Until this fact is established, the eleemosynary motive remains dormant.

One example of "conditional altruism" is the gift of money to purchase bullet-proof vests for a police department. Even if a corporation's executives are thoroughly convinced of the life-saving urgency of that equipment, the dollars probably will not leave the corporate treasury until the decision-making executives foresee a symbiotic benefit such as favorable press.

The executive director of the Atlantic Richfield–sponsored foundation declared, "We believe we ought to set an example to persuade other corporations and corporate foundations to expand their support of nonprofit organizations." Well and good— but before money was committed to implement that noble policy, you can bet that the potential gain to the donor was analyzed and understood.

The Great Debate: Should Corporations Give?

We have been examining why corporations give. The more fundamental and controversial "why" question is, Why should corporations give in the first place? Because the issue sparks heated debate, you as a grant-seeker at least should be aware of the polarized viewpoints of the adversaries.

In Favor of Corporate Philanthropy—The chairman of the board of Mobil Oil Corporation wrote:

> Business cannot flourish if the community it serves is deteriorating.

The chief executive of another *Fortune* 500 company recently told us:

> Corporations make their profits from society and therefore have a moral philanthropic obligation to it.

These pronouncements by top corporate officers are not new. Long ago the Bank of America founder, A. P. Giannini, declared:

> A business must share its prosperity with the people it serves. That's not a matter of choosing. It's a natural law.

Enlightened self-interest is another frequently-heard rationale for corporate philanthropy. What is good for American society as a whole benefits the business community because, the argument goes, corporations can better maximize their profits in a healthy society.

It is no secret that the business community has long criticized the government's third-sector (nonprofit area) funding as being wasteful and ill-directed. Many executives believe that corporate philanthropy gives the business community a chance to do it its way. And if all corporations were to donate the legal maximum 5% of their pretax earnings, corporate-derived funding would be a monumental alternative to government funding.

Another oft-voiced belief is that since the nonprofit sector needs the support of corporations, the latter should respond.

Some funding authorities believe that the very act of corporate philanthropy has a hidden salutary effect on our society: The exercise of selecting funding recipients sharpens a corporation's awareness of public needs.

Against Corporate Philanthropy—As one corporate PR director confided to us,

> Business social responsibility is a hollow phrase that quickly became endeared to the hearts of the practitioners of our trade. It provided us with a much needed euphemism.

Another PR officer advised not to give much credence to those quotes by corporate presidents that extol the company's unselfish philanthropic spirit. To paraphrase her, "It's a bunch of Barnyard Stuff."

Not all corporations can be charged with making barnyard statements. Aetna Life & Casualty asserted:

> We believe our greatest potential for impact is through our everyday business. Our first obligation must be to run it well and responsibly, for without this, nothing else is possible. Through our business we can affect the lives of millions, often in a very significant way.

A number of socio-economists also are convinced that business can serve society better in the long run by curtailing donations. They believe the resulting maximized profits can, in part, be reinvested to achieve a host of far-reaching gains for the general public.

Reinvestment helps create growth and as a by-product, more and better-paying jobs, which in turn lower the cost of governmental unemployment programs. Growth also stimulates the local economy.

The dollars can be invested in employee-related programs that improve training, salaries, fringe benefits, safety and general working conditions. The community's disadvantaged minorities and the handicapped can be served with Equal Opportunity hiring and training programs.

Consumers score when some of the profits are recycled into improved product-testing and safety programs, into more substantive warranties and repair services, and into prompter and more responsive replies to legitimate complaints.

Employees and the community alike reap rewards when the plant or office building is more aesthetically designed or landscaped. The same is true when a corporation decides to renovate an historically significant building rather than demolish it. A variation on this theme occurred when an elevator company convinced the owner of a landmark Park Avenue building in Manhattan to preserve by rehabilitation the existing classic elevator carriages rather than to install modern ones. The lift manufacturer did this despite the fact that it would have earned a larger profit if it had installed new elevators.

The community benefits when the corporation invests in better environmental protection equipment. Which corporation is more socially responsible—the one that generously supports the local symphony orchestra while neglecting to install a waste purification system needed to cut down on the pollutants contaminating the community's rivers and skies, or the corporation that uses its dollars to do the opposite?

Through reinvestment, a manufacturer may develop a better dialysis machine, surgical tool, or whatever, that may save lives or cure the ailing. Even though the corporation makes its profit, the results of its research and development help people just as much as if a nonprofit organization developed that machine. As has happened many times in the past, the corporation can benefit society more than the nonprofit organization if the corporation—through higher efficiency—can research, develop, and/or produce the equipment at a lower cost despite the built-in profit.

Opponents of corporate philanthropy point out that besides reinvestment, there are two other options in using the money saved by axing charitable contributions. One option benefits the stockholder, the other the consumer.

The money can go to stockholders in the form of higher dividends (if the funds are reinvested, the stockholder still gains through equity appreciation). As Milton Friedman, the celebrated conservative economist, argued in his book *Capitalism and Freedom,*

> Few trends could so thoroughly undermine the very foundations of our free society as the acceptance by corporate officials of a social responsibility other than to make as much money for their stockholders as possible.

This feeling was echoed in the *Fortune* magazine quote of a dissenting stockholder:

> Don't make any charitable deduction contributions . . . . give us higher cash dividends so we can make contributions to whomever we want.

She raised an interesting issue. Does the corporation have the legal or moral right to force the stockholder to make involuntary contributions (perhaps to causes she does not support) when that money would otherwise be hers? If one accepts her business philosophy, then a corporation should not give away funds unless it can justify to the stockholder that the contribution will prove to be at least a break-even investment.

Whatever the legal or ethical answer may be, a Conference Board study of relatively large corporations found that negative reaction by stockholders to corporate philanthropy was virtually nil. Whenever stockholder-dissidents raised this issue, they seldom garnered the support of more than 3 percent of the total stockholder vote. Did this result from stockholder apathy or from the ability of the management elite of large, widely-held corporations to hold tight reins on the corporate decision-making apparatus? Probably a little of both.

Some vehicles for marshaling stockholder concern exist. One is *The Corporate Examiner,* published by the New York–based Interfaith Center on Corporate Responsibility. This newsletter keeps readers apprised on actions by church groups against social-responsibility injustices that they deem to have been committed by specific corporations.

It is worth noting that when a corporation decides to opt for the stockholder-dividend or the reinvestment-equity route, its taxes go up because of the absence of the charitable deduction. This usually means that the tax bite on the average American will be less severe and/or that the government will have more funds to carry out its social service programs. To put it another way, a corporation that makes charitable deductions forces the average American taxpayer to give more and/or the government to cut back its programs.

The last of the three options for using the charitable dollars that are lopped off the corporate budget is to give the money to consumers in the form of reduced prices.

Another battlefront of the corporate philanthropy debate is whether corporations are the best, most knowledgeable, and most efficient conduits for charitable dollars. After all, corporate philanthropy opponents opine, corporations are structured to make money, not to give it away. Since most corporate contribution executives are not professionally trained philanthropists, they may fund projects without a perspective or long-term plan and so do more harm than good by, for instance, unwittingly forcing a more-qualified nonprofit organization to cease operations by supporting a lesser-qualified one.

Corporate-philanthropy antagonists also worry seriously that as business-derived philanthropy expands in size and influence, it will seek more controls over the programs and thereby impair the objectivity of and execution by those who manage the programs. The argument that a corporation does not have influence over a program if it gives the money with "no strings attached" is tenuous because the very decision as to whether to sponsor a project or to renew funding constitutes selection power. And with the propensity of corporations to fund time-tested, no-risk projects, fledgling nonprofit organizations do not receive their fair share of the tax-supported corporate charitable dollar.

Know to Whom
Corporations Give

Corporate Vs. Total-Private Giving

As the following table indicates, corporate-giving patterns differ from those of overall private giving.

	CORPORATE GIVING	TOTAL PRIVATE GIVING*
Religion	—	46.5%
Health and Welfare	38.3%	23.8%
Education	35.7%	14.0%
Culture and Art	9.0%	6.3%
Civic Activities	11.5%	2.9%
Other	5.5%	6.5%
	100.9%	100.9%

Source: *Giving USA 1979 Annual Report.*
* Includes contributions from corporations, foundations, bequests, and individuals.

The most obvious dissimilarity between the two sources is in the area of religion. Corporations almost totally leave the funding of religious institutions and projects to their employees and their families. If you seek money for a religious cause, the message is clear: Look for funding from individuals, from bequests, or even from independent foundations—not from corporations or company-sponsored foundations.

Corporations give a higher relative percentage of their total philanthropic dollar (38.3 percent) to health and welfare than does private giving as a whole (23.8 percent). Corporations are selfishly aware that the funded health-and-welfare activities benefit their employees.

A similar contrast in corporate versus private giving occurs in the categories of education and civic activities, but not for the same primary reason noted above for health and welfare. Corporations generously support higher education principally because colleges and universities help train their future key personnel. And they actively fund civic activities because that munificence helps build good community relations.

Corporate Contributions by Recipient Category

Who receives the corporate philanthropic dollar? According to a survey conducted by The Conference Board of 814 large companies, the relative percentage figures for 1977 were as follows:

Health and Welfare

Federated drives: e.g., United Ways	21.6
National health agencies	0.8
National welfare agencies	0.9
Hospitals	
Capital grants	4.0
Operating grants	0.9
Employee matching gifts for hospitals	*
Youth agencies (e.g., Boys Clubs, Boy & Girl Scouts, YMCA)	3.2
Other local health and welfare agencies	4.2
Capital grants excluding hospitals	—
Subcategory not identifiable	2.6
Total health and welfare	38.3[a]

Education

Higher education institutions	
Unrestricted operating grants	5.9
Student financial aid (funded through college or university)	2.1
Departmental and research grants	5.3
Capital grants (including endowment)	5.2
Employee matching gifts for education	3.8
Grants to state and national fund-raising groups	1.8
Pre-college educational institutions	1.1
Scholarships and fellowships (other than those reported above)	3.1

Education-related organizations	2.3
Other	2.6
Subcategory not identifiable	2.5
Total education	35.7

Culture and Art

Music	1.3
Museums	2.0
Public TV/Radio	1.6
Arts Funds or Councils	0.8
Theaters	0.6
Cultural Centers	0.9
Dance	0.1
Libraries (other than academic)	0.3
Employee matching gifts for culture and art	*
Other	0.6
Subcategory not identifiable	0.8
Total culture and art	9.0

Civic Activities

Community improvement	4.4
Environment and ecology	2.5
Justice and law	0.5
Housing and urban renewal	0.5
Research organizations, other than academic (e.g., Brookings, CED, etc.)	1.2
Other	1.7
Subcategory not identifiable	0.7
Total civic activities	11.5

Other

Religious activities	0.3
Groups devoted solely to economic education (e.g., Joint Council on Economic Education, Junior Achievement, etc.)	1.3
Groups in U.S. whose principal objective is aid to other countries	1.0
Activities other than above	2.6
Subcategory not identifiable	0.3
Total other	5.5
Dollars not identifiable because donee is unknown	—
Grand Total	100.0

* *Less than 0.1 percent.*
ᵃ *Subcategory percentages do not add up to this total because of rounding.*

The category that has recently been experiencing the greatest jump in percentage is Culture and Art, thanks particularly to the missionary endeavors of the Business Committee for the Arts.

Federated Campaigns

Roughly one third of the country's corporate-contribution dollar does not pass directly into the hands of the intended recipients. It first travels through philanthropic go-betweens such as

> Corporate Theatre Fund
> National Catholic Charities
> National Corporate Fund for Dance
> National Merit Scholarship Corporation
> United Jewish Appeal
> United Negro College Fund
> United Way

The last member on our list, United Way, is the largest and most prominent of them all and has become the subject of heated debate. Many nonprofit agencies accuse it of virtually monopolizing the payroll deduction method of raising money from corporate employees. Another oft-heard complaint is that the local United Way organizations are too conservative and tradition-bound in the selection of funding recipients. While sometimes these attacks on the United Way are manifestations of the sour grape syndrome, in many cases they are legitimate.

Federated fund-raising organizations promise their participating fund-seekers more success for lower cost and less effort. In most cases, they deliver.

Individual Recipients

To a whopping extent, corporations prefer to contribute to tax-exempt organizations rather than to individuals, for the reasons we have outlined in Key Five, "Know Thyself." That Key will also show you why you should not necessarily be discouraged by the corporate philanthropic bias toward tax-exempt organizations, since there is a way to circumvent that obstacle. If you are seeking a scholarship or fellowship, you should also read Appendix C, "Student Aid," p. 170.

Know What Corporations Give

The check (cash) is the best known and most obvious mode of corporate contributions. Business firms also give nearly as much, if not more, dollar value to charitable causes in the various forms of gifts-in-kind (noncash) contributions, a characteristic that makes corporate philanthropy different from that of foundations and most governmental agencies.

Cash

The cash donation can be unrestricted (e.g., for use as general operating funds) or more likely, can be earmarked for specific purposes such as endowing a professorial chair or funding a scholarship. Sometimes the corporation is fully or partially compensated for its donation; a block of tickets to a ballet performance and a special medical service for its employees are examples.

One variant of the cash donations is financial aid. For instance, the Woonsocket Institution for Savings loaned $385,000 at submarket rates to the Ocean State Performing Arts Center of Providence, R.I. Eastman Kodak was even more generous, giving the Rochester (N.Y.) Museum and Science Center the interest on a $900,000 fund for ten years (the full control of the money reverts to Eastman Kodak at the end of that period). Another company, through its Cummins Engine Foundation, lent the

Region Ten Mental Health Foundation of Columbus, Ind., $10,-800 for emergency funding to tide it over until it received a Federal grant check. Of course, if you ever want an interim-funding loan, you will have to furnish conclusive evidence that the funds are forthcoming. Virtual certainty is not enough.

Company Materials

Even though the Tax Reform Act of 1969 eliminated or hamstrung many of the tax advantages previously allowed for donations of materials to charities, the current laws still offer tempting incentives to most corporations. If the recipient has tax-exempt status and the materials are not yet fully depreciated on the books, the corporation can take an immediate as opposed to a delayed tax deduction for the undepreciated value of materials that are of little or no value to it. Even if the materials are fully written off the books and the recipient does not have tax-exempt status, the corporation will probably save money by giving the materials outright because it will save future storage and bookkeeping costs. The corporation could, of course, gain the same saving by throwing the unwanted material on top of the dump heap, but—despite what cynical corporation-watchers fancy—most executives would rather see it end up in the hands of a nonprofit organization than let it go to waste.

To give you an idea of the wide variety of materials that corporations donate, we have researched and compiled the following itemized list. In spite of the obvious absence of delectable assets such as petty cash and postage stamps, our shopping list may make you drool.

Addressing machines	Attaché cases
Adhesives	Audio-visual equipment
Air conditioning units	Automobiles
Aircraft	Auto supplies
Artist supplies	Ball-point pens
Athletic equipment	Barrels

Batteries
Bicycles
Binoculars
Blackboards
Bleachers
Blowtorches
Blueprint equipment
Boats
Boilers
Bookkeeping forms
Books
Book shelves
Boxes
Bricks
Brushes
Burglar alarms
Buses
Calculators
Cameras
Carbon Paper
Cement
Chairs
Chemicals
Circuit breakers
Cleaning equipment
Cleaning supplies
Clipboards
Clocks
Closed-circuit television
Coat racks
Collating machines
Computer hardware
Computer software
Curtains
Darkroom equipment
Desks

Drills
Duplicating equipment
Electric cord and wires
Electric heaters
Electric motors
Electric switches
Engines
Envelopes
Environmental-control devices
Fabrics
Fans
Fiberglas
File cabinets
Fire-fighting equipment
First-aid supples
Flashlights
Food
Food preparation equipment
Food service equipment
Furnaces
Fuses
Garbage bags
Garbage cans
Gardening equipment
Gasoline and oil
Gas tanks
Generators
Glass
Gloves
Hammers
Hand trucks
Hard hats
Hardware
Headphones
Hoists
Hoses

Humidifiers
Hydraulic equipment
Incinerators
Inks
Insecticides
Laboratory equipment
Ladders
Lathes
Lift trucks
Light bulbs
Lighting fixtures
Linoleum
Lockers
Locks
Looseleaf binders
Loudspeakers
Lubricants
Lumber
Magnifying glasses
Mailing machines
Maps
Marine equipment
Medical equipment
Metals
Meters
Microphones
Microscopes
Mobile homes
Motor scooters
Musical instruments
Nails
Nuts and bolts
Offset equipment
Optical equipment
Paging equipment
Paintings

Paints
Paint sprayers
Paper cups
Paper towels
Partitions
Pencils
Pencil sharpeners
Photocopying machines
Photographic film
Plants and flowers
Plating equipment
Podiums
Polishes and waxes
Polishing equipment
Portable buildings
Postage machines
Postage scales
Printing equipment
Public address systems
Pulleys
Pumps
Radar equipment
Radios
Refrigerators and freezers
Roofing materials
Rope
Rubber stamps
Rugs
Rulers
Safes
Safety goggles
Sanding machines
Saws
Scaffolding
Scissors
Screwdrivers

Sewing machines

Shelving

Signs

Sinks and tubs

Snow removal equipment

Soaps and detergents

Soldering equipment

Spotlights

Stage equipment

Stools

Stopwatches

Storage cabinets

Surveying equipment

Switchboards

Tables

Tape

Tape recorders

Tape measures

Telephone-answering machines

Telephone equipment

Telescopes

Televisions

Telex equipment

Thermostats

Tiles

Timecard equipment

Tires

Toilet paper

Transformers

Trucks

Truck trailers

Typewriter ribbons

Typewriters

Uniforms

Vacuum cleaners

Vending machines

Video recorders

Walkie-talkies

Water coolers

Water softeners

Waxing machines

Welding equipment

Wheelbarrows

Work benches

Work clothes

Wrapping paper

Writing paper

X-ray equipment

If it is against the policy or disposition of the corporation to give you substantial equipment, on the order of a truck, ask if it will loan the equipment to you. Some do.

Timing can be a crucial factor. Your chances of receiving used office furniture dramatically increase, for instance, when a company is relocating. Often the company considers that relocation is the apropos time to replace its old (but for your purposes, still useful) furniture with new equipment.

Another timing-related opportunity for you occurs when a company is ceasing operations. Creditors willing, you may be able to pick up some needed materials—as did the police department of Newport, R.I., which received a closed-circuit television camera free from a store that was going out of business. The equipment, we were told, has already caught someone allegedly stealing valuables out of parked cars.

Companies such as cosmetic firms often give sample-sized products to nonprofit organizations conducting events such as charity balls or dinners. Reason: The product will enter the hands of opinion-makers, the type of people who normally attend such functions. And since the product reaches their hands in the context of a charity-oriented gift, the donor receives invaluable goodwill.

Fund-raising auctions are another repository for donated corporate goods (and services). The higher the quality and size of the audience, the more likely it is that the corporation will give.

Advertising and Promotion Services

Some corporations will sponsor a print or broadcast media advertisement on your behalf.

Perhaps you have noticed a large department store in your area taking out a newspaper ad that appeals for the public's financial support or extols the virtues of a local community-service group. Assume that the ad costs $1,000. The key issue is whether the nonprofit organization would have been better off receiving $1,000 cash rather than receiving the benefits of the ad. In most cases, the answer is no. In the short-term, the advertisement can bring in more than $1,000 worth of contributions, volunteers' time, and/or other forms of community support. Moreover, the long-term credibility and financial health of the nonprofit organization can be improved through the increased public awareness generated by the ad. From the donor's point of view, the $1,000 gift in the form of an advertisement gives the charitable act much more visibility than if the donor simply handed over a check.

Sponsored advertisements for charity can give the donor another benefit. Mobil Oil frequently buys advertising space in the editorial pages of *The New York Times* in order to present its issue-oriented messages. When a representative of the Boy Scouts asked if Mobil would donate the space for an advertisement promoting the Boy Scouts' cause, Mobil said yes—with good reason. Above and beyond Mobil's desire to serve a worthy cause, the company knew that the donated ad would create a warmer public feeling for any future Mobil institutional ads. In other words, the donation helped diminish the public's growing reaction of "oh, there's another self-serving ad by that oil company."

A particularly creative example of sponsored public-service advertisements was the one placed by the Syntex Corporation in the *Palo Alto Times.* This one-page ad featured twenty clip-out coupons, each of which spotlighted a nonprofit organization along with the details on how the public could support it.

Corporations are not the only source for free advertising and promotion for your organization. Some advertising agencies, public relations firms, and promotion houses volunteer their services to nonprofit organizations. These companies can assume the entire job from creation through execution or can handle one or more facets of the overall project, such as letting one of their graphic artists help you prepare a slide presentation. From time to time we have come across agencies looking for a nonprofit organization to help, either gratis or for a reduced fee; so if you are in need of their services, it does little harm to ask for help whenever you happen to meet an executive of an advertising, PR, or promotion agency.

Public-service announcements (PSAs) are free air-time given to nonprofit organizations by commercial radio and television stations to fulfill one of their obligations to the Federal Communications Commission. Several national firms can help you to create, disseminate, and place your PSAs in broadcast outlets, as well as in such other media as newspapers, magazines, and mass-transit posters. For further information on PSAs, write The Advertising Council (825 Third Avenue, New York, N.Y. 10022), The Public Media Center (2751 Hyde Street, San Francisco, Calif. 94109), or The National Association of Broadcasters (1771 N Street NW, Washington, D.C. 20036).

Other Company Services

Besides advertising, PR, and promotion, there are other company services worth tapping, including accounting. The prestigious accounting firm of Touche Ross, for example, has provided free service to some of the small, struggling art groups. Also investigate whether you can use these company services:

Communications	Photocopying
Data processing	Photography
Financial planning	Printing
Legal	Secretarial
Mailing	Transportation
Personnel management	Writing

If the company cannot provide the services, inquire if it can get one of its retained agencies to do the work for you free or at cost. Remember, the company is sometimes in the position to "twist the arm" of its suppliers.

Try to start a chain reaction. This principle was illustrated in the case of a group that developed an inner-city garden. The group received free seeds from a seed supply company, which in turn convinced one of its customers, a nursery, to donate the time of its staff to teach youngsters how to plant and grow the seeds. Then the nursery was able to get one of its suppliers, a garden tools manufacturer, to donate hoes to the project.

When accepting the donation of the services of a corporation or its agencies, you must be prepared for the eventuality that an unforeseen crisis or business opportunity will readjust the donor's priorities. For example, a new-product breakthrough may require the publicity department to work overtime, leaving no time for you. One of the best ways to insure yourself against this type of setback is to schedule as much lead-time as possible.

Company Personnel

A valuable asset for your organization is the talent, knowledge, expertise, technical skills, contacts, and just plain sweat of the people who work for corporations. This pool of personnel consists of individuals from all corporate levels, from file clerk to top executive.

A few corporations, including IBM and Xerox, have established executive-loan programs through which you get the use of the individual's time and the corporation foots the salary bill. Although competition for loaned executives who will work for you full-time is understandably keen, getting an executive to work for your project several hours a week on the company payroll is not a long-shot proposition. The higher one is in the corporate hierarchy, the greater the number of on-payroll hours he or she is likely to give. A Conference Board study found that 92 percent of the several hundred top executives surveyed work for charities on company time.

If you cannot get the company to pay for the employee's time, try to get the employees to volunteer on their own. Do not be hesitant about asking corporate executives to donate their time. After all, volunteerism is a firmly entrenched American tradition: About forty million of us do it—some for less than altruistic reasons. Volunteering often accelerates careers; some corporations go so far as to make it a tacit condition for executive-level promotions, because they want their management team to cultivate close ties with community leaders.

Side benefits of recruiting executive volunteers are that they may become financial contributors, that they may get other people within the corporation to volunteer and/or contribute, and that they may be instrumental in spreading favorable word-of-mouth about your organization within the corporate walls.

If an executive turns you down, you still may come out ahead if you ask him or her for introductions to other executives who may be willing and able to volunteer. Unless you ask, you will never know. From the refusing executive's point of view, such referrals do not cost money—at least, not in the short term (the executive later may be asked to contribute to your organization by the recommended executive who subsequently became one of your volunteers).

What is the optimum number of volunteers? "As many as possible" is not always the judicious answer, because sometimes a cohesive, dedicated squad of volunteers can produce more than a disorganized, semi-inspired army.

The avenues of access to volunteers within a corporation are usually controlled by the firm. Try to get the corporation to pave your way by giving you promotional announcements in house organs and on bulletin boards or by allowing you to set up a card table at the entrance to the employee cafeteria or lounge. The stronger the corporation's implied or stated endorsement of your project, the more success you will achieve.

A more direct road to fund-raising is to get the corporation to help you entice employees into giving you money rather than time. Better yet, perhaps you can get the corporation to collect the money for you by installing and staffing a strategically-placed donation booth or if you are extremely fortunate, via a payroll deduction program. The latter path is hard to travel because it is defended tooth and nail by its current overlords, the United Way and a few other federated fund-raising campaigns.

Company Facilities

You can save rental fees charged by hotels and other space-renters if you can get a corporation to allow you to use its facilities for your board meetings, workshops, presentations, and other gatherings. Variations of this approach include space for working, storage, and window displays. And by gaining the space, you have placed the proverbial foot in the company's door.

The hours and days a corporation and a nonprofit organization need facilities such as conference rooms, auditoriums, and employee eating and recreational areas are usually out of sync,

which is good. Corporations typically use their facilities from
9:00 to 5:00 on workdays, whereas many nonprofit organizations
prefer to schedule evening or weekend meetings in order to maximize attendance.

If you are fortunate, the corporation will commit these facilities to you on an on-going basis—the third Tuesday of every
month from 6:00 to 8:00 P.M., for example. But more likely, the
company—for sake of retaining needed flexibility—will not reserve the space for you too far in advance, especially if the schedule takes place during normal business hours.

Company facilities can also be used for special events such as
art exhibitions or fund-raising events. A creative example occurred when Pan Am allowed a charity to hold a fund-raising
cocktail party inside the then novel and newsworthy twin-storied
Boeing 747. Department stores relish introducing their new facilities with a bang to the local opinion-makers by having charities throw fund-raising parties within them. Macy's of Kansas
City, Mo., for instance, gladly donated the use of its new kitchen-
ware department as the site of a benefit for the local Folly
Theatre.

Do not just think in terms of your using corporate facilities—
reverse the situation. For instance, if you have unscheduled time
for your conference room and a corporation plans to rent the
same type of hotel space for a seminar, ask the corporation if it
will pay you a comparable fee or the equivalent as a donation for
the use of your facilities. Before greedily adding up the dollars in
your mind, be sure your charter and the applicable tax laws
allow you to rent space to commercial firms.

Matching Funds

This fund-raising mechanism provides incentive for you and
contribution leverage for the corporation. It works like this: For
every dollar you raise, the corporation will give you one or more
dollars according to the agreement. Most corporate matching
funds have predetermined deadlines and dollar ceilings and are
awarded on a dollar-for-dollar basis—although sometimes the

ratio can be as high as 3:1, as with Exxon. In the past, institutions of higher education have cornered nearly all the corporate matching-fund dollars, but other funding areas such as the cultural arts and medical research are starting to make headway. Education is not suffering, however, because the number and magnitude of corporate matching-fund programs are on the rise.

You do not always need to raise cash to satisfy your side of the matching-fund equation. A few corporations will accept the equivalent value of goods, services, and other gifts-in-kind.

One of the biggest growth areas in matching funds is the employee sector. For each dollar an employee gives to a qualified tax-exempt organization, the corporation agrees to give an equal or greater amount to the same organization. To illustrate, the Allied Chemical Corporation matches gifts of up to a maximum of $1,000 per year per employee. Other corporations, such as Monsanto, set the limit at $5,000. In these situations it pays to get employees to donate to your organizations, because the multiplier factor comes into play. When pitching those people for funds, emphasize the leverage argument, that is, the fact that they will be able to double or quadruple the mileage of their charitable dollars.

Sometimes the employee does not even have to contribute cash to your organization to qualify for corporate philanthropic dollars. An increasing number of companies have programs to donate money to those tax-exempt organizations that are supported by the donated hours of company employees. Perhaps "matching contributions" would be a better name for this variant of the matching-fund concept. "Challenge grants" is the euphemism sometimes used by fund-raisers who believe that that phrase is more enticing to the executive's way of thinking than "matching funds." Either appellation works.

Other Forms of Corporate Aid

Bulk Purchasing—If your organization makes large purchases of a particular item, such as business envelopes, typewriter ribbons, or pencils, or plans to buy a new truck, you may be able to prevail upon a corporation that purchases those items in money-saving bulk quantities to buy extra ones and then sell them to you at the reduced cost. You thus buy the supplies at the super bulk-rate without having to buy in wholesale lots.

Guaranteed Order To Get Project Under Way—This concept can be best illustrated by the device used by an organization that was unable to persuade an automobile dealer to either donate or sizably discount a car for its raffle. Undaunted, the charity secured the assurance of a local corporation that it would purchase $1,000 worth of the raffle tickets. With this commitment in hand, the dealer acquiesced. The company, by the way, made good use of the tickets: It gave them to its workers in the spirit of good employee-relations.

Loss Insurance—It is possible to get a corporation to subsidize your fund-raising event by guaranteeing to absorb all or part of any loss you may incur.

Underwriting Business Travel Costs—At times corporations agree to pay all or part of the cost for one of your staff to attend an important out-of-town conference, seminar, convention or workshop.

Subcontracting—A corporation often may find it acceptable and even necessary to subcontract to an organization like yours part of a contract it received from a governmental agency.

Subscription List—The Hugh M. Heffner Foundation loaned, free of charge, *Playboy* magazine's subscription list to the Chicago Symphony Orchestra. Think of similar opportunities that may match your needs.

Training Programs—Corporations can give your constituents on-the-job training.

Student Aid—Corporations often finance scholarships, either independently or through the National Merit Scholarship Program. They also participate in Junior Achievement programs.

Discounts—Many corporations are willing to sell you their goods or services at a money-saving discount. While this policy is not necessarily in the realm of philanthropy, it does save you money.

Know How
Corporations Give

How Corporations Differ from Other Funding Sources

To understand corporate giving, it is useful to know how it differs from other types of philanthropy. First, for the sake of perspective, let us examine the annual magnitude of corporate giving in relation to the four other major funding sources:

Governmental Agencies	$100 billion
Individuals	$33 billion
Corporations	$4 billion
Bequests	$3 billion
Foundations	$2 billion

The $4 billion corporate estimate is ours—it includes the $2 billion that corporations take as charitable tax deductions and the $2 billion worth of gifts that are written off as business expenses. The $100 billion governmental-agencies figure is the researched estimate published in one of our companion books, *The Art of Winning Government Grants*. The remaining three estimates—for individuals, bequests, and foundations—are the 1978 calendar-year estimates published in the authoritative *Giving USA* booklet.

We know a number of people who strike out in corporate fund-raising even though they have expertise in obtaining grants from governmental agencies and independent foundations. While a noncorporate background is extremely useful, corporate fund-raising is in several major ways a different ball game requiring new knowledge and strategies.

For openers, few corporations are staffed with professional money-givers, unlike some foundations and virtually all governmental agencies. More often than not, corporate philanthropy is a part-time activity for executives whose primary career goal lies elsewhere, be it in public relations or in personnel management.

Nor do the vast majority of corporate philanthropic programs operate with the well-designed guidelines that are hallmarks of most large, independent foundations and nearly all governmental funding sources. Corporate giving is usually more informal—in fact, corporate philanthropists enjoy more person-to-person contact and less-formalized communication with the prospective donees than do their counterparts in governmental agencies and independent foundations.

Because most corporate executives by training and inclination like to make their judgments expeditiously, their decision-making system tends to give you a faster yes or no answer. One successful corporate fund-raiser confided to us that once he has put his best foot forward, he tries to get the corporation to say yes or no quickly, thus saving the frustration and often the cost of waiting for a protracted verdict.

The average size of a corporate grant is several hundred dollars, whereas that of independent foundations is several thousand dollars. The average figure for government grants is even higher. On the other hand, corporations can give gifts-in-kind (see Key Three, "Know What Corporations Give").

Compared to individual giving, corporate philanthropy is less emotional. You may be able to induce your fellow townfolk to give from their heart solely in response to a tear-jerking photograph of an abused child, but the corporate executive must be more analytical.

IRS statistics indicate that the charitable deduction of the average individual is 3 percent (out of a legal limit of 50 percent) of the adjusted gross income. In comparison, the charitable donation taken by the average corporation is 1 percent (out of a legal limit of 5 percent) of its pretax earnings.

Bequests are a horse of a different color. Unlike with funds garnered from corporations and most other sources, the decision as to who receives the money tends to be resolved years if not decades before the check is ultimately delivered to the donee. And once the benefactor departs the planet Earth, the decision is virtually irrevocable. With bequests, you have to do your sales work early—very early.

The Corporate Philanthropic Conduits

Corporations have three basic philanthropic conduits. They can give the cash or gifts-in-kind as a

1. Tax-deductible charitable donation
2. Standard business expense
3. Grant through company-sponsored foundations

Some corporations make use of one conduit while others put to advantage two or all three.

CONDUIT 1—TAX-DEDUCTIBLE CHARITABLE DONATIONS

Most people think of this conduit when they think of corporate philanthropy. Be it cash or gifts-in-kind, the corporation can take a tax deduction for the contribution (provided, of course, that you are a tax-exempt organization). The maximum amount a corporation can legally deduct in a year is 5 percent of its pretax income.

CONDUIT 2—STANDARD BUSINESS EXPENSE

For every philanthropic dollar corporations claim as a tax deduction, they channel another dollar to the nonprofit world under the banner of the standard business expense. Few people realize that Mobil Oil and a number of other large corporations often choose to underwrite PBS television programs, special museum exhibitions, and other services for the common good out of public relations, public affairs, advertising, and other nonphilanthropic-department company budgets. This is no different from a corporation sponsoring a commercial rock concert, as some do. The costs are treated as business expenses and accordingly are deducted from pretax earnings.

There can be advantages for the corporation in taking the business-expense as opposed to a charitable-deduction tack. It can aggressively promote its participation (such practice for charitable donations is normally proscribed by law or protocol). Also, a corporation can camouflage sizable philanthropic spending from stockholders who might otherwise object. From the company accountant's viewpoint, the deduction for a business expense reduces the tax bite just as much as one for a charitable contribution—and it has no 5 percent ceiling. From the recipient's viewpoint, both types of dollar have the identical purchasing power.

A number of corporate outlays are made for operational reasons yet end up helping worthy causes as much or almost as much as if philanthropy were the original aim. Profit-oriented investments for programs that train exconvicts or unemployed ghetto teenagers are examples. Also, consider the upward trend in the last decade of corporations purchasing art works to decorate offices, hallways, and lobbies. Except for the purchase of schlock art and the like, the money spent for these paintings and sculptures usually benefits deserving artists. TIP: If you are such a person, introduce yourself to some of the commercial interior-decorators in your locale.

CONDUIT 3—THROUGH ITS COMPANY-SPONSORED FOUNDATION

Approximately 1,500 of America's 22,000 grant-making foundations are sponsored by corporations (and/or by individuals such as executives and family members closely associated with corporations).

According to the *Foundation Directory #7*, in a recent year the top 20 company-sponsored foundations, along with their grant totals (in thousands of dollars), were the following:

	GRANTS *	FOUNDATION NAME
1	$10,381	Ford Motor Company
2	7,237	Atlantic Richfield Foundation
3	6,146	Alcoa Foundation
4	5,504	United States Steel Foundation, Inc.
5	5,422	Xerox Fund
6	5,354	Exxon Education Foundation
7	4,910	Procter & Gamble Fund
8	4,778	Mobil Foundation, Inc.
9	4,777	Minnesota Mining and Manufacturing Foundation, Inc.
10	4,769	Gulf Oil Foundation of Delaware
11	4,754	Eastman Kodak Charitable Trust
12	4,584	Amoco Foundation, Inc.
13	4,460	Dayton Hudson Foundation
14	4,202	Monsanto Fund
15	4,124	General Motors Foundation
16	3,939	General Electric Foundation
17	3,935	General Mills Foundation
18	3,842	Exxon USA Foundation
19	3,823	Shell Companies Foundation, Incorporated
20	3,054	BankAmerica Foundation

* Includes all charitable contributions except loans.

Technically, company-sponsored foundations are legally distinct from the corporations, but for all practical purposes, they are not autonomous, as are the classic independent foundations. A good illustration of the difference between company-sponsored and independent foundations is the comparison between the two similarly named 501 (C) 3 organizations, the Ford Motor Foundation and the Ford Foundation. The Ford Motor Company of today sponsors and controls the first but contributes nothing to or has any suzerainty over the second.

A number of significant differences exist between the typical company-sponsored and independent foundation. First of all, the company-sponsored foundation funds causes closely linked to the financial interest of another entity—the donor corporation. The ratio of grants to assets is usually much higher for a company-sponsored foundation because more often than not, it serves more as a channel for than as a repository of funds. The average company-sponsored foundation donates more grant dollars and is more willing to answer letters of inquiry than its counterpart. Finally, a company-sponsored foundation has the unique advantage of being able to call upon the services, facilities, and management expertise of its benefactor, a corporation.

The number of company-sponsored foundations has grown nearly 100-fold since 1938, from 19 to the present total of some 1,500. The largest number of company-sponsored foundations were created during World War II and the Korean War, when the excess-profit tax rate was as high as 82 percent. By forming foundations, corporations were able to keep control of some of the money rather than let it seep into the government coffers. The number of company-sponsored foundations and their financial impact started to decline following the enactment of the Tax Reform Act of 1969, although this downward trend began to reverse itself in 1976. In contrast, the number of independent foundations has been declining in recent years.

What manner of corporations have foundations? The larger the corporation, the greater the chance that it will have one. The same is true if the corporation is experiencing a steady, pronounced growth in profits.

Today slightly over half of the *Fortune* 500 industrial giants sponsor their own foundations. When a corporation does have a foundation, most of its philanthropic dollars usually flow through its nonprofit, tax-exempt organization.

Why do corporations found foundations? First and foremost, perhaps, are the tax advantages. With a foundation a corporation can save on taxes by transferring to the foundation most of its corporate philanthropic dollars during years of high earnings, when the tax bite is the severest, and by doing the opposite during lean years. Another tax benefit occurs when the IRS disallows deductions for gifts made to recipients residing outside the United States; by directing the largess to the foundation, which in turn makes the gift, the corporation can take the deduction.

Yet another advantage is stabilization of the corporate philanthropic program by eliminating the roller-coaster effect of business cycles. A corporation, through its foundation, can grant a constant $2 million a year even though—because of economic fluctuations—it can afford to give $3 million one year but only $1 million the next year. Nonprofit organizations that must rely upon steady, sustained funding appreciate this variation of hedging.

A foundation, by its very existence, helps reduce some of the pressure that a substantial customer could bring upon, say, the vice-president of sales to support the customer's pet charity. With a foundation, the executive is better able to sidestep the funding request assault by insisting, "It is a foundation and not a company decision."

There are other byproduct benefits to having a foundation. Because the word "foundation" has a favorable connotation among the average citizenry, the corporation gains PR value. Moreover, because the presence of a foundation often encourages the corporation to take a longer-range view of its philanthropic programs, better management usually results.

From the corporation's board of directors vantage point, two self-serving rewards accrue. One has to do with power: With a foundation, relative control of the philanthropic dollars usually lies less in the hands of the executives and more within the influence of the board members. The second benefit involves ego: Many corporate board members quickly accept the invitation to serve simultaneously on the foundation's board because, in their minds, being directors of a foundation elevates their stature in the eyes of the public and their social peers.

Many times, all or most of the key individuals of the foundation also serve as company employees or directors. In theory, these dual-positioned mortals carry out their functions independently of one another. In practice, however, those binary-roled players more often than not view the foundation's needs and goals from the company's perspective.

To illustrate this partisan duality of responsibilities, let us see how the twelve key officials of the Cummins Engine Foundation relate with the sponsoring corporation, the Cummins Engine Corporation. According to the most recent Cummins Contributions Report, their dual roles were as follows:

INDI-VIDUAL	HIS/HER FOUNDATION POSITION	HIS/HER COMPANY POSITION
1.	Chairman of the board	Chairman of the board
2.	Vice-chairman of the board	Vice-chairman of the board
3.	President; board member	President; board member
4.	Secretary/treasurer; board member; executive director	Director: corporate contributions
5.	Board member	Executive vice-president; board member
6.	Board member	Vice-president: personnel
7.	Board member	Chairman of the executive and finance committee; board member
8.	Board member	Executive director: public policy
9.	Board member	Board member
10.	Board member	Vice-chairman of the executive and finance committee; board member
11.	Administrative officer	Manager: contributions administration
12.	Senior Program officer	Manager: corporate contributions

Most corporations prefer to give this overlapping responsibility a low profile, but others do the opposite. For instance, Levi Strauss and Company freely states that its foundation "is staffed by the Company's Community Affairs Department."

Even when a corporation has a foundation, it never funnels all of its philanthropic contributions through that body. The principal reason why the corporation sometimes funds from its own corporate treasury is to avoid jeopardizing the tax-exempt status of its foundation, since some gifts so obviously self-serve the corporation that they would violate existing laws governing foundations. An example would be a donation to a university research laboratory that was developing a product that possessed profit potential for the corporation.

How Corporate-Giving Programs Differ

No two corporate-giving programs are alike. This section will outline some of the major ways they differ.

By the Administrating Department—Sometimes the department is a distinct entity within the corporate structure; other times it is abyssmally buried within another department, such as personnel, or within the president's office. Our research has uncovered a wide variety of names for the corporate subunit that administers philanthropic matters. These designations include the office or department of

> Community affairs
> Community relations
> Community sources
> Contributions
> Corporate communications
> Corporate social responsibility
> Corporate support
> Philanthropy
> Public relations
> Urban affairs

The individuals in charge of these areas are variously called administrators, chiefs, coordinators, directors, heads, managers, officers, special assistants, and vice-presidents. These administrators, however, do not necessarily make funding decisions on their own, as that is normally reserved for a committee.

By Who Makes the Decision—Decision-making power can be concentrated in the hands of an individual or, at the other extreme, can be diffused throughout a complex network of committees. Philanthropic contributions of most medium- to large-size corporations are voted on by a single three-to-seven–member contributions committee typically comprising a cross section of corporate disciplines, such as personnel, PR, consumer affairs, and so forth. For most if not all of the committee members, philanthropy work is only a part-time endeavor; their major company roles lie elsewhere.

Committee participation can be decentralized on the local-plant or worker level—or it can be firmly rooted in the offices of the top-echelon executives. In the latter case, the vast majority of the people who control the corporate-philanthropic purse strings are white, male, middle-aged, and closely linked to other members of the power structure through club memberships, college ties, old friendships, and mutual economic interests. This homogenized power clique has been a prized target of social reformers, who point out that without proper representation on the committee by women, ethnic minority members, youth, and ordinary citizens, there will be a myopic and reactionary view of a community's needs.

The degree of power of the committee varies from rubber-stamp to omnipotent status. In most cases the committee's decision is binding, although formal approval may be required from a higher authority, such as the president, if the amount is relatively large.

By Type of Company—Contributions as a percentage of a company's domestic pretax net income do vary by industrial classification. Here are the 1977 figures based on a Conference Board survey of over 500 large companies:

PERCENT OF PRETAX INCOME	INDUSTRY
1.22%	Banking
1.22	Business services
0.71	Chemicals
0.57	Electrical machinery and equipment
0.41	Engineering and construction
0.96	Fabricated metal products
0.44	Finance

0.68	Food, beverage, and tobacco
0.45	Insurance
0.60	Machinery, nonelectrical
1.23	Merchandising
0.82	Paper and like products
0.67	Petroleum and gas
0.96	Pharmaceuticals
0.87	Printing and publishing
0.94	Rubber and miscellaneous plastic products
0.68	Stone, clay, and glass products
0.28	Telecommunications
0.60	Textiles
0.49	Transportatio..
0.35	Transportation equipment
0.29	Utilities

Also, according to a 1977 Conference Board survey, there are differences in the giving patterns of manufacturing and nonmanufacturing firms. The latter gave a higher percentage of their contribution dollars to health and welfare programs (47.5 percent vs. 33.9 percent) and to United Way (31.2 percent vs. 19.4 percent). Manufacturers, on the other hand, gave a higher percentage to education (40.2 percent vs 25.5 percent). In the cultural-and-arts area, nonmanufacturing companies held the edge (10.1 percent vs. 8.4 percent). There was no appreciable difference in the civic-program area (11.8 percent vs. 11.5 percent in favor of the manufacturers).

There are other giving traits. The more labor-intensive the company is, the more it probably will contribute to health and welfare causes. The likelihood and magnitude of giving to grass-roots-type projects escalates for those firms, such as banks and large department stores, that are deeply entrenched in and dependent upon a community. Among the corporations least likely to give to any type of cause are those firms such as exporters whose dialogue with the public is so indirect that a philanthropic investment would earn scant PR mileage.

By Profit-and-Loss Trend—Corporations that are experiencing stagnation and, especially, a decline in profits will generally contribute a lower percentage of their pretax income—partially to cut costs, and partially to prevent stockholder and employee malcontent. It is a thankless task to try to justify donations to charity while your stockholders are receiving lower dividends (with a corresponding drop in the market value of the stock) and your employees are being denied pay hikes or even being laid off.

By Commitment—According to IRS data, only one in five corporations reported tax-deductible gifts on their income tax returns. Some corporate critics frequently quote that statistic to support their contention that 80 percent of the companies are, if you allow our euphemism, "scrooging the public." If truth be told, that statistic is misleading because most of the nation's corporations are "ma and pa" operations whose principals largely prefer to give as individuals. Few of them resemble the miserly character in Charles Dickens's *Christmas Carol.* The overall national corporate average of the percent of pretax income that is written off as charitable deductions is 1 percent although some firms proudly donate the full 5 percent legal limit. Dozens of firms in Minneapolis have formed an exclusive 5 Percent Club; their most celebrated member, the Dayton-Hudson Corporation, was the subject of a Harvard Business School case study on philanthropy.

By Funding Focus—Some corporations prefer to give a large number of small gifts to a broad selection of recipients in the belief that "everyone" will be satisfied. Other corporations concentrate their philanthropic thrust. As an official of Control Data told us,

> We prefer a strategy of direct involvement, investing our combined financial, technological, and organizational resources in specific major efforts, rather than a strategy of more widely dispersed cash philanthropy.

By Size of Company—The larger the company, the bigger its philanthropy budget and the larger average size of its grants will likely be. However, the smaller the company (so long as it has at least 25 employees), the more it probably will give in terms of percentage of pretax income.

By Sophistication of Management Systems—A handful of corporations have exemplary management systems for their philanthropic programs. They have well-thought-out goals and judge proposals accordingly; they thoroughly investigate the proposed project and the applicants by, for instance, consulting outside experts and making on-site visits; they evaluate the results of the completed project; they periodically review their funding priorities and objectives. Most corporations, on the other hand, lack a master plan—a haphazard approach that seems rather ironic in light of the professional standards these corporations otherwise impose on their profit-making departments.

By Quality of Management Personnel—A number of corporate philanthropic managers were assigned their duties in ways that would shock most management consultants. In the words of one personnel director, the current contributions manager was pigeon-holed into his slot because "our company doesn't know what else to do with that ineffective but loyal and lovable ole chap." A small but growing number of corporations are seeking individuals who can competently assume contributions responsibilities—and in order to attract the right person, those companies are willing to pay a salary commensurate with the responsibilities.

Know
Thyself

Know Your Goal

You now know why, to whom, what, and how corporations give. But that is not enough—you must also clearly know your goal. Amazingly, few grant-seekers have a vivid perception of exactly what they wish to accomplish. To help you define your own goal, ask yourself the need-related questions that evaluators often ask themselves when they evaluate proposals. You will find these questions on page 111, in the "Need" section of Part Two.

There are many benefits to properly identifying your goal. To begin with, if your goal is ambiguous, how in heaven's name will the corporation comprehend it? Odds are the corporation will misconstrue your goal and will be unable to determine whether your aim is compatible with its objective. Just as important, an ill-defined goal reveals much about your competence.

Before you can develop rationally the components of your proposal, such as methods and budget, your goal must be accurately set forth. Otherwise those components will not be logical outgrowths of your true objective.

Another reason for precisely defining your goal is to help keep your organization from unwittingly compromising its objectives in order to get funding. Organizations that bend their goals to fit the needs of the corporation may win the battle (short-term money) but usually will lose the war (long-term effectiveness and a clear conscience).

Down-the-line misunderstandings between you and the corporation are minimized by goal clarity. So are personnel conflicts within your organization.

Unless your goal can be stated in a brief paragraph or two, you are probably still groping for the right description. Goals requiring a long exposition usually are still uncrystallized. If you are having trouble articulating your goal, write down on paper what is in your mind, even if your initial thoughts are jumbled. Writing helps uncloud these thoughts, as does showing your drafts to your colleagues to gain their fresh comments and suggestions.

Know Your Specific Needs

Make an inventory of your needs, listing them in order of priority, be they cash or gifts-in-kind. To spark your gifts-in-kind thinking, glance over our "shopping list" on pages 23–26.

Itemizing your needs will improve your grant-seeking quest because corporations usually find it more advantageous to give particular rather than general support. This is exemplified by the success of a museum that received a Mobil grant to pay the cost of one of its projects—keeping its doors open with free admission one evening a week. If the museum had requested funds to defray its general operating expenses, the likelihood of success would have been substantially lower because that alternative would have given Mobil's gift less visibility.

Another instance illustrating the merits of itemizing one's needs occurred in a medium-sized Southern city in which a community service agency determined that it needed more space for its accounting department. Instead of paying the expense of leasing additional facilities, it freed one of its rooms that housed important though infrequently consulted records by persuading a next-door corporation to store the file boxes, gratis, in one if its vacant rooms.

Know Your Strengths and Weaknesses

Being human, it is impossible for us to see our pet projects with total objectivity. What is within our capability is being reasonably objective, a status that can be obtained only if we analyze with hard-nosed detachment our strengths and weaknesses. Many grant-seekers, for instance, have been severely smitten when they ultimately discovered that the abilities, reputations, resolve, and tenacity of certain staff members fell short of expectations. These fund-raisers would have been better off if they had tried at an early stage to find the answer to questions like these: How qualified are the staff members to perform the required tasks? Will enthusiasm wane? How substantial are the staff's contacts with outside individuals and organizations whose cooperation is vital to the project's success?

In determining your strengths, attempt to discover your "unique selling proposition," a Madison Avenue phrase that defines those products or services that you can offer better than your competitors to a particular audience, be it the corporation or your project's beneficiaries. Make no bones about it—you are in competition for the limited number of corporate philanthropic dollars, and the more you can pinpoint your unique value, the more successful your fund-seeking campaign will be. To determine your unique selling proposition (USP), survey individuals beyond as well as within, your organization. Outsiders, being disinterested, are often in a better position to see your organization as it really is.

Know Your Chances of Success

Corporate fund-raising programs almost always consume considerable money and time. Before burying yourself in the researching and proposal-writing tasks, ascertain whether your project stands at least a fair chance of being funded from the corporate sector. Your fundability decreases if

You are an individual or a non-tax-exempt organization. It is a fact of life that unless you are a student seeking financial aid or are an organization with an Internal Revenue Service Letter of Exemption, your chances of receiving funds directly from corporations and their foundations are bleak. The primary reasons corporations prefer to donate to IRS-sanctioned tax-exempt institutions is because such status virtually guarantees the allowability of the tax write-off and the legitimacy of the organization as a recipient. This latter motive is particularly important to corporate foundations because both the foundation and its officials are subject to fines if the recipient uses the money for purposes such as influencing governmental legislation. (See Appendix D for details on how to apply for tax-exempt status.) Do not necessarily terminate your quest for corporate funds if you are an individual or if you are an organization that has not yet received tax-exempt status. You have an alternative. Convince an existing tax-exempt organization of the merits of your project and ask it to be your administrator. The corporation is protected because the check goes to an eligible recipient, which in turn hands over the money to you, minus perhaps 5–10 percent to pay for the cost of administering your program. Include that expense in your budget.

You are politically oriented. Corporations may quietly give you money to help sway legislation or elect candidates, but not via the route of a charitable donation.

You appear to be antibusiness or antiestablishment. Few people like contributing to their own destruction.

Your project is potentially controversial. Practically no corporation wants to be associated with projects that may become nightmares for their public relations department.

Your project is risky or untried. Corporations love backing winners, not losers.

You want to make a profit. Except in a few cases, such as funding minority enterprises, corporations do not invest their philanthropic dollars in capitalistic endeavors.

Your field is not a philanthropic priority. Statistics verify that religious groups receive scant corporate philanthropic support.

Almost but not quite as meager are corporate donations to precollege-level educational institutions.

You are looking for the wrong type of funds. Most corporations prefer not to support ongoing projects that require a long-term funding commitment, be it based on a contractual or a moral obligation. Nor do most corporations fancy having their donations being used for general operating expenses and building construction projects.

You are geographically undesirable. It is a basic law of physics that as the distance between two objects doubles, their mutual gravitational attraction decreases fourfold. This law can be loosely applied to corporate fund-raising. The farther your project is from the corporate operations, the less attractive you are.

You seek too big a grant. It is not uncommon for large-sized independent foundations, and especially governmental agencies, to give megasized grants that are measured in hundreds of thousands if not millions of dollars. Less than 10 percent of the grants awarded by medium-sized corporations reach $1,000. Even in the case of the average *Fortune* 500 corporation, the under-$10,000 grants predominate. Only a handful of behemoth corporations render titanic gifts, and then usually only to recipients such as PBS or the United Way. Should your funding needs be larger than a corporation's policy allows, ask the firm to pick up part of your action.

Your project is not timely. Perhaps your project is passé or premature for the corporation.

You lack lead time. We know instances where grant-seekers have had checks handed to them before their first meeting with the corporation was completed. Do not count on these fortuitous encounters—they are few and far between, as nearly all corporate fund-raising endeavors require ample lead time. Although securing philanthropic funds from corporations typically takes a shorter period than from foundations and governmental services, you still must plan on four to twelve months between your first contact and (if you are successful) the receipt of the check. The time span will be even longer if you are out of sync with the timetable of a corporation that plans its philanthropic program and gifts well into the future; in that case, you are trying to get a piece of next year's budget. Do not fret over a situation that forces you to plan far in advance, because most grant-seekers lack the inclination, discipline, and foresight to do it, and thus the competition for those particular dollars is less keen than for grants in general.

Some grant-seekers do not even exhibit midrange planning, preferring to knock on the corporate doors for eleventh-hour funding to put out fires. If you wait until you see smoke, you will not only decidedly diminish your chances of funding, you will also create a bad impression with corporate executives, who by training and talent are people who plan ahead. When they see an individual or a nonprofit organization fail to plan adequately, they seethe. The message is clear: Develop your fund-raising as an ongoing part of your activities by devoting time to it on a year-round basis, not just when you need the funds.

You lack the wherewithal. Grant-seeking can cost money—lots of it. Unless you have the reserves to launch a well-prepared campaign, think twice first. You will be in competition with numerous other fund-seekers, many of whom will be large-scale cultural or educational institutions with sophisticated tools at their disposal. To appreciate how the demand for the corporate philanthropic dollar outstrips the supply, consider the fact that the aggregate requests for dollars to most corporations approaches or exceeds their corporate profits.

You lack a track record and credentials. If your organization is new, you obviously have no track record and thus have two strikes against you. This means that you must be much better than a well-established fund-seeker just to be able to compete with it evenly. If the Boy Scouts of America were founded yesterday instead of in 1910, it would—because of its newness—have to fight tigerishly for corporate support. This is not fair to fledgling organizations, but that is the way it is and you cannot change it. One way to get around this Catch-22 dilemma is to emphasize the accomplishments of your staff and board of directors. You will need to convey more than their enthusiasm, since relevant credentials are what count most. For example, your executive director's twenty-year hitch as an administrative vice-president of a respected bank is insufficient qualification by itself for him or her to head a drug rehabilitation center, no matter how heartfelt the personal commitment. What happens if your organization is new and the people within it lack convincing credentials? In that case, you should not be looking for corporate funds in the first place.

We cannot emphasize too strongly the short-sightedness of accepting a project that you and your organization are less than 100 percent qualified to undertake. Some nonprofit organizations take on a host of projects in order to augment their influence and employee count. This is a brazen manifestation of bureaucracy in action. If the organization is as truly people-oriented as it professes to be, then the organization will turn down a project if its efficiency in carrying out its other projects would be jeopardized. Likewise, it will reject the project if it believes that another organization could do it better.

Research/Research/ Research

There is no way getting around it—if you want to be successful at corporate grant-seeking, you must do your homework. The depth of your research, naturally, will be largely dependent upon the magnitude of the prize you are seeking.

Organize Your Resources

Before initiating your research of the corporations, it is imperative for the sake of optimum productivity that you first organize your resources, a labor that in itself involves research. You must do the following:

> Design a master plan.
> Develop contacts.
> Identify your information sources.
> Establish an information system.

DESIGN A MASTER PLAN

Small-scaled grant requests need not have elaborately-designed master plans. This is especially true in the case of individuals, because of factors such as cost-effectiveness. A large-scale grant-seeking project involving a number of people, on the other hand, should have a detailed plan of action so everyone concerned will work toward the same goal. Otherwise, they may be toiling at cross-purposes because of misunderstandings, power conflicts, or other success-impairing predicaments.

A good plan will clearly state the objectives and each person's authority and responsibility. Ideally, one key member of your organization should be designated the coordinator in title or function; that individual will facilitate sound intra-organizational communications by serving as the central clearinghouse for any pertinent information dealing with grant-seeking projects. The master plan must be realistic in what the organization and each person in it can do, and it should explicitly set forth the budget and a timetable that takes into account unforeseen but likely setbacks and delays.

DEVELOP CONTACTS

Almost mandatory in corporate fund-raising is having influential supporters, people who can persuade or at least open the door to those who sit within the philanthropic circles of power. Your contacts can also serve you as an intelligence network alert to new opportunities and changes in the corporate philanthropic winds. If you do not already have your quorum of well-placed contacts, start cultivating them *now* rather than just before you need them, as most grant-seekers do.

Some of the contacts you need are (or should be) sitting on your board of directors, as these individuals are one of the best if not the best vehicle for enlisting the cooperation of business leaders in your community.

Since business executives are usually more responsive to the philanthropic requests of people within their own industry, your board's composition should be broadly based. In the most ideal of circumstances, your board would include the presidents or chairpersons of the largest, most successful, and most respected local firms in such diverse fields as manufacturing, banking, retailing, and law. Each board member would in turn pitch your cause to his or her colleagues via a letter, telephone call, or meeting, or perhaps in the form of a group luncheon.

Of course, a well-selected board collectively should give you more than contact value. Your organization can benefit from their wisdom, expertise, and prestige—and perhaps through more mundane but still beneficial ways such as providing the use of their secretaries' skills, their companies' mailing-room equipment or telephone tie-line service, their clubs' meeting rooms, etc.

Members of your board also constitute a monetary wellspring in themselves. Being a millionaire is no longer as exclusive a club as it was years ago. According to a study released by the U.S. Trust Company, the country had over 500,000 millionaires as it entered the 1980 decade. Taking into account the expected population increase, national economic growth, and inflation, we conservatively extrapolate that figure into a total by the mideighties of a million millionaires. Yes, a million millionaires.

One way to convince reluctant prospects to come aboard is to emphasize that according to the Filer Commission report, 92 percent of the chairpersons and company presidents surveyed actively participate with at least one nonprofit organization . . . and that 55 percent were active with five or more organizations . . . and that each executive donates an average of six hours (half company time, half personal time) to charitable organizations.

Other appeals that have been used to entice a prospect to join the board include the inherent challenge, the change of pace from the normal responsibility, the opportunity to meet and work with other influential community business and social leaders (most top executives welcome this exposure) and last but not least, the chance to do a good deed.

Just as important as knowing how to ask prospects to join is knowing who not to ask. Board members who do not deeply believe in your cause or who are willing to lend their names but not their time can be counterproductive.

Getting executives to serve on your board is not the only way to plug into their ring of contacts. Ask them to serve as a volunteer. When trying to persuade executives to volunteer, remind them that most corporations want their executives to participate in community causes and that, therefore, volunteering can further one's career.

Among the types of executives who have the strongest urge to volunteer are those who have recently relocated to the community and so need avenues for developing new friends and acquaintances. An equally fertile source for volunteers is the large number of unemployed spouses of these corporate nomads who seek alternatives to idle hours spent at home.

Without knowing it, you may already have one or more volunteers who work for the corporation. These individuals can prove to be most instrumental in pitching your cause within the corporate walls. This was the case with a fresh-air fund that perused its records to identify those corporate executives who, under its fresh-air program, were inviting disadvantaged inner-city kids to their country homes. Most of those executives were more than willing to write letters to or speak before their company's contributions committee.

Obviously, the most potent contacts to court are the people within the corporation who make the funding decisions. More about them later. Other contacts worth developing include the leaders in your field, elected and appointed governmental officials, trade union representatives, key purchasers of the corporation's goods and services, and stockholders (if the company is small and closely held).

Once you have cultivated a contact, ask him or her for a written letter of endorsement—you cannot have too many of these testimonials, which bolster your credentials. Another benefit is that by inducing the contact to commit in writing his or her belief in your project or organization, you help emulsify that person's allegiance, giving it added consistency and permanence.

Equally as important as cultivating contacts is to disarm "anticontacts," that is, your existing or potential adversaries who may badmouth you or otherwise undermine your project for any of various reasons. Perhaps one of your antagonists is an old enemy on real or imagined grounds, is a supporter of one of your rival organizations, or is someone who will lose something if your project is funded. For instance, if the money enables you to improve your services to your constituency, your counterpart on the other side of town may fear that its organization will appear deficient because it cannot offer the same service. Defuse these bombs before they explode by starting today to try to open and maintain a constructive dialogue with other organizations and influential individuals who may be directly or indirectly affected by your project.

IDENTIFY YOUR INFORMATION SOURCES

You will find in Part Four a compendium of third-party information sources—select those that are relevant to your particular needs. There is also the most direct data source of them all, the corporation itself.

We wish we could tell you otherwise, but the act of obtaining information on philanthropic matters from most corporations is more often than not a frustrating if not an impossible process, as most companies are reluctant to reveal their "private matters," for one or more of the following reasons:

Fear of being besieged by applicants
Concern over encroachments on the cherished tradition of corporate privacy
Qualms about stockholder disapproval
Apprehension of being stung by muckraking activists or journalists
Desire to maintain utmost flexibility
Lack of recognition of the grant-seeker's need for the information
Possession of hazy or nonexistent contribution policies and guidelines

One of the most frequently heard of the unconvincing apologies from corporations that do not publish adequate material is that they are "contemplating a change in policy for next year."

Can you imagine these same companies refusing to give their customers informative sales literature because they are "anticipating a price change for next year"? Sometimes it is not that a corporation is purposely withholding the facts you need; it may be that the company has never compiled the data in the first place.

When a corporation does publish documents reporting its philanthropic and/or social responsibility programs, the printed word is usually short on substantive details and long on rhetoric.

A surfeit of corporate-contribution executives convey an attitude in this vein: "What more could you want? All the answers you require are contained in our offset information sheet." Regrettably, quite often your and the corporation's idea of the definition of "sufficient relevant data" will differ.

Paucity of detail can occur even when a corporation produces a lengthy and seemingly comprehensive report. For example, a senior vice-president of the Shell Companies Foundation told us that its booklet, *Pattern For Giving,* "describes everything we do in some detail." While we appreciate Shell for publishing its 38-page booklet, we as corporate grant-seekers need to know more facts than the names of the recipients. Shell did not tell us the size of the grants; nor did it tell us in more than vague terms the purposes of the grants.

Another illustration of insufficient facts is Mobil's 32-page booklet on its grant recipients in the arts sector. Although Mobil, laudably, furnishes the names of the grant-winners and brief descriptions of the funded projects, it neglects to tell us how much each recipient was awarded, a statistic that helps grant-seekers evaluate giving patterns. In contrast, Exxon's glossy, magazine-style *Dimensions* publication was more enlightening, as it conveyed a more detailed account, including the dollar figures, for each donee receiving $5,000 or over. Since Mobil and Shell obviously had the exact amounts at their fingertips, why did they withhold them?

Of even less value to grant-seekers than the corporations' literature on philanthropic activities are their annual reports. Only a minute percentage of annual reports give meaningful facts that allow the prospective donee to make rational deductions about grant policies and guidelines. Those reports, however, can help you ascertain profits, products, and the like.

Rhetoric seems to be the stock-in-trade for most corporate philanthropic promulgations, as our readings of corporate social-responsibility reports have verified. Many of these publications open with phrases such as "What's good for society is good for business and the well-being of both sectors is intertwined." Balderdash. One of these booklets subtly boasted of its philanthropic good deeds and had the unmitigated gall to conclude the publication by casually remarking, "The activity presented in the previous pages was intended to inform, certainly not to try to impress you." One of the best and most useful summaries of corporate giving policies was published by the Equitable Life Assurance Company (see Appendix B, page 168).

Sometimes the information you seek is published and available, but the employee with whom you are speaking is unaware of its existence. When requesting philanthropic literature, therefore, be sure you are listening to the right source within the corporate maze.

Also, be as specific as possible on what you want and ask for the answers of vital questions that you anticipate will be lacking in the published material. This tactic forces the corporation to supplement its correspondence with a custom (or, perhaps, a modified "boilerplate") letter that can be more accurate, up-to-date, and informative than its generalized published material. Also ask the corporation to put you on its permanent philanthropic-subject-matter mailing list, should it have one. If, after doing your preliminary research, you do not know to whom the request should be sent, mail it to the "Office of the President."

ESTABLISH AN INFORMATION SYSTEM

One of the most tedious yet most indispensable of tasks in fund-raising is developing and maintaining a workable information-gathering, -storage and -disseminating system. This step is crucial to your ultimate success whether you are an individual or a megastaffed organization, because if you do not have the needed facts and reasoned conclusions at hand, you cannot make the best decisions as to whom to approach for funds and how to do it.

For the various reasons stated above, securing the needed information from the corporate world is often difficult at best. But since in this field some information is usually better than none, you cannot fall back on the lame excuse, "What's the use?"

The first rule is to assign one person the responsibility and authority to serve as the central repository of the gathered intelligence. That individual should be the person performing the grant coordinator's role that we mentioned earlier.

One of the principal duties of the coordinator will be to start (and/or to develop access to) a grant-seeking reference library that will contain, within budgetary limits, all the pertinent reference sources described in Part Four. Since no two grant-seekers' needs are identical, each grant-seeker's reference library should have a unique composition. Some will be measured in inches, others in shelves.

When establishing your library, avoid pitfalls such as designing a needlessly complicated reference system that thwarts easy access on the part of your colleagues. Outdated information and a lack of up-to-date information are other common shortcomings, particularly if the grant-seeker is involved in a less than large-scale fund-raising campaign. It takes time and money to operate an efficacious library, but the question you must ask yourself is whether you can afford not to make these investments. In the vast majority of cases, grant-seeking reference libraries suffer more from stinted expenditure than from extravagance.

As important as a good reference library is good internal communications. The coordinator should discuss the project as early as possible with all the personnel concerned. Summary notes on the key aspects of all meetings should be written and circulated—and to foster new ideas and constructive criticism, feedback must be encouraged.

Key-account Analysis

One of the most ill-contrived grant-seeking campaign strategies is shotgunning, a scatter-attack on the corporate treasuries that we frequently see employed by neophyte and experienced fund-raisers alike. Also immensely disquieting to us is the large number of grant-seekers who inadequately research their prospective donors before sauntering into the corporate executive suite. We are disturbed by the lack of professionalism because if grant-seeking is to be cost-effective, the finite time and resources available to the grant-seeker must be concentrated on obtaining funds from his best prospects as determined through methodical research. "Key account analysis" is the sales executive's term for this procedure.

Your first step is to do some preliminary research and brainstorming to create a list of your best bets, perhaps twenty-five or so in number. Then, by researching those corporations in depth, abridge the list to about ten firms. Digging even deeper and wider, augment your research findings on those "finalists"—and you are now ready to zero in on those corporations on a one-on-one basis without undue risk of blowing the opportunity or wasting your time barking up the wrong tree because of insufficient intelligence about a corporation.

WHAT TO LOOK FOR

To research a corporation properly, you must uncover a large and varied assortment of facts and insights.

Grant Patterns—Scrutinize the past gifts of the corporation. To whom did the gifts go? For what purpose? In what dollar amounts in terms of average and range? Was the geographic scope of these gifts local, regional, and/or national? The closer your project resembles the previously funded projects, the closer you are to the corporation's treasure chest.

Distance from and Magnitude of Business Activity—The philanthropic dollar seldom strays far from its corporate home, be it an office, a warehouse, or a factory. And the faster and stronger the business pulse beats, the greater the corporate philanthropic budget is likely to be. You can almost predict the location and relative importance of a business unit by examining an itemized list of its donees.

Funding Guidelines—What are the corporation's funding objectives? What are its priorities? What type of project does it prefer not to fund? What type of projects are flatly ineligible? (For instance, some corporations will not or cannot give to United Way recipients if the corporation is currently contributing to that federated fund-raising agency.) Does the corporation have restrictions on the size and geographic scope of its grants? Does the corporation donate gifts-in-kind? Does it make matching gifts? When is the budget formulated? When is the submission deadline? To whom should the proposal be sent? When is the decision made? When are the funds dispersed?

Funding Vehicle—Are gifts made through a company-sponsored foundation or the company per se? Are the gifts treated as a charitable deduction or a standard business expense?

Decision Making—Where is the decision made? Who makes the decision? What are their names, titles, addresses and telephone numbers? What criteria are used? (for a working list, see "Questions Evaluators Ask," page 109).

Leadership Match-Up—Do any of your personnel or contacts know any key official at the corporation?

Corporate Statistics—Find out facts such as assets, sales, profits, and employee count, since these statistics may indirectly help you estimate a philanthropic budget that may be cloaked in secrecy. Also determine the rate of profit growth, because accelerated increases usually mean corresponding quantum leaps in next year's philanthropic budget.

Curveballs—The playing field of corporate grant-hunting whizzes with unexpected curveballs that can harry if not bean researchers. For example, some announced budgets have not yet been officially approved, while others may be suddenly and drastically curtailed without notice or explanation. Some grant patterns can be misleading because of an irrational grant-giving motive: for instance, a nonprofit organization in the town of Ithaca, N.Y., may receive a sizable grant from a Chicago-based corporation because the latter's founding president attended Cornell University. General Motors has more than one company-sponsored foundation containing the corporation's name. The titles of the foundations of some other corporations are dissimilar to the names of their sponsors. Who would expect *Playboy* magazine's foundation to declare women's rights one of its funding priorities? Our list of illustrations could go on, page after page.

What the Corporation's Competition Is Doing—Enhance your ammunition arsenal by determining what projects have been funded by your prospective patron's competition. Having researched these facts, you can diplomatically mention to your potential donor, in so many words, that "XYZ Corporation gave $50,000 to sponsor a summer concert in the park and we were wondering whether . . . ?"

Your Competition—"Go where the money is" is a shopworn fund-raising maxim that should not be followed blindly, because some corporations receive several hundred requests per month, ten to twenty per business day. This pathetically skewed balance between supply and demand often obliges the decision-makers to play the role of the Almighty in determining who among many qualified applicants is to be rejected. If every other grant-seeker is attempting to pluck the produce from the same corporate orchard, the collective competition may be so keen that the cost of harvesting may exceed the fruits of your labor. If so, look elsewhere.

Besides assessing the amplitude of your competition, try to find out the specific nature of the other projects similar to yours that the corporation is reviewing for possible funding.

Armed with this knowledge, you will be in better stead to position the uniqueness of your project.

Corporate Fact Sheets

If you are collecting data on several or many corporations, we advise you to create a standard form for organizing the gathered information. Our suggestion becomes practically a necessity if you plan to disseminate the intelligence to a number of people.

Design your format to suit your particular needs but be sure to have headings that will encompass such vital categories as the funding vehicle (corporate or foundation); existing contacts; the decision-makers and -influencers along with notable background facts about them; insightful financial and personal statistics; significant philanthropic policies and guidelines, including application deadlines; donation budget and gift range in dollars; details on recently funded projects similar to yours; a précis of your preliminary strategy, including a brief summary of the reasons why you believe the corporation should and will fund you. Be sure also to note possible obstacles and how they can be overcome.

Keep your fact sheets as concisely written as possible and leave ample white spaces in and around the text for subsequent modifications and marginalia by you and your readers.

Circulate each completed fact sheet to the appropriate people involved with your grant quest, asking them for their constructive criticism. Just as important, ask your readers (especially your influential ones, such as your board of directors) if they have any potentially useful contact of any sort with the sway-holding corporate officials. To stimulate their memory cells, attach to the fact sheet a brief bio of each of the pertinent corporate officials—perhaps the match-up will be a college tie, a religious affiliation, a blood relationship, a membership in a club, or a shared avocational interest. The best all-around source for this biographical data is usually one of the *Who's Who* editions, although *The Social Register* and some of the other references listed in Part Four can also prove to be invaluable.

Researching Company-Sponsored Foundations

This volume is not a book on the ins and outs of obtaining foundation grants because, as we have previously noted, the policies of nearly all company-sponsored foundations merely echo the philanthropic and business objectives of their sponsoring corporations. These subordinate institutions do not make their decisions with the same nonprofit detachment as do most independent foundations. Except for the germane tax-exemption provisos that we have already mentioned, a company-sponsored foundation should be approached more in terms of being a corporation than a foundation, despite its formal IRS 501 (C) 3 status.

Moreover, the subject of foundation grant-seeking is a distinct, full-scale discipline so vast and complicated that it would require an entire book to cover the topic meaningfully. We draw your attention to this volume's companion book, *The Art of Winning Foundation Grants,* as well as to other foundation-oriented publications and services described in Part Four.

Develop Creative Tie-ins

A number of years ago the Filer Commission delivered a now-famous quote:

> Corporate giving is the last major
> undeveloped frontier of philanthropy.

We believe that otherwise-perceptive statement would be more accurate if the word *unexploited* were substituted for *undeveloped*. The amount of funds being obtained from corporations is largely unexploited because in their pursuit of the corporate dollar, the preponderance of grant-seekers use the same fund-raising strategies and techniques designed for raising money from governmental agencies and independent foundations. While there is some overlap in the procedures used to raise money from corporate and noncorporate sources, several major differences exist, variance of shattering significance is the emphatic need for the grant-seeker to devote much more of his or her mental energies to the development of creative tie-ins.

Developing creative tie-ins simply means discovering ways that your project can simultaneously serve your and the corporation's selfish interest (without, of course, jeopardizing the integrity of your organization). This approach has long been used by businesses to increase their sales by symbiotically linking their efforts on a special project with those of another business—

in the executive's parlance, it is usually called a marketing or promotional tie-in.

These tie-ins occur daily throughout our land, from Maine to California. One nationwide example is the Hertz-Ford deal, whereby Hertz agrees to make statements in its rent-a-car ads such as "Hertz features the exciting Ford Fairmont" in return for a better price deal on the cars it purchases.

Since well-conceived creative tie-ins can produce direct or indirect profits for the corporations, there is no limit, theoretically, to the maximum amount of funds corporations could be willing to dole out to charity, whether in the form of tax-deductible contributions or business expenses. Too many writers in the fundraising field choose to ignore or play down that fact. Instead, they argue that the way to increase the flow of corporate dollars to the nonprofit sector is to make corporations more aware of their philanthropic responsibility. This strategy begs the issue, because the debate still rages over whether corporations have that responsibility in the first place. A more pragmatic solution to inspire corporations to enlarge their munificence to the nonprofit world is to increase the appeal to the corporate profit motive through more and sounder creative tie-ins. We believe the time is ripe for more nonprofit organizations to avail themselves of this opportunity.

Reverse Roles

You have already completed your first step in the development of creative tie-ins by inventorying your needs as we suggested in Key Five, "Know Thyself." Your second step, now, is to reverse roles by asking yourself, "In which ways can a corporation selfishly benefit from our project? How can we modify our project (without sacrificing our integrity or results) so that it can better satisfy the corporation's objectives?"

Do not just think in terms of increasing the direct profits or sales of the corporation. Also analyze how your project might improve the firm's relationships with its various special publics:

customers, stockholders, employees, trade unions, journalists, community business and social leaders, government officials, corporate competitors, and others.

Examples of Creative Tie-ins

To set your imagination in motion, we have assembled several dozen creative tie-ins that have been put into action by your fellow grant-seekers. Perhaps our list will enable you to conceive "variations on a theme" or will trigger your mind into envisioning an entirely new and exciting, never-tried-before concept. We hope so.

The Cooper-Hewitt Museum needed money to help defray the costs of its special exhibit on shopping bag art. Who would you solicit? The museum knocked on the door of a paper bag manufacturer, with pleasing success.

Boston's National Shawmut Bank gave away thousands of free museum memberships as an encouragement for people to open new or increase their existing accounts. The project was broadly successful and the bank, the depositors, and the participating museums all benefited.

Many entrepreneurial-minded artists in need of work and money have secured commissions from corporations to create paintings or sculptures to decorate the firms' lobbies, reception rooms, hallways, and offices. We know of one instance in which an arts professor, in need of a project for his sculpture class, solicited and received a commission from a local plant that wanted a sculpture to beautify its facilities. To increase the appeal of his offer, the professor promised that the artwork would relate with the products made in the plant. Another inventive variation of the arts-for-business concept occurred when R. J. Reynolds Industries agreed, for public relations reasons, to sponsor an art photography contest in its corporate home state of North Carolina. Subsequently, it even purchased some of the artwork for use in its offices.

Oil companies frequently support environmental protection programs for less than altruistic reasons. For example, they often fund marine-oriented projects because of their corporate vulnerability to public outcry over oil spills. Atlantic Richfield and the Cousteau Society have enjoyed a multiyear relationship, while the Standard Oil Company of California, together with its Chevron family of companies, has poured money into the Woods Hole Oceanographic Institute.

A theatre group received financial aid from a local tobacconist to stage a play featuring the pipe-smoking Sherlock Holmes.

In Louisville the Kentucky Opera Association agreed to present a free performance for the families of the employees of the Brown-Forman Distillers Corporation as partial repayment for a $40,000 gift from the firm. Next door, in Indiana, the Indianapolis Symphony Orchestra has given four complimentary tickets to each corporation donating $25 or more. In New York the Metropolitan Museum of Art thanked Mobil for its financial support by giving it free, hard-to-get King Tut exhibition tickets for use by the company's employees.

Where did Chicago's Museum of Science and Industry go for funds for its "The Money Center" exhibit? A local bank (Continental), of course.

A federated black-college campaign successfully won a sizable grant from a major automobile manufacturer. A well-placed source confided to us that while the ostensible reason that the drive received the funds was that the corporation wanted to support the campaign for purely eleemosynary reasons, the truer, unpublished reason was more complicated and less altruistic. The U.S. government was on the corporation's back to have it increase the number of blacks holding middle-management positions. The corporation was unable to fill the suggested quota because an insufficient number of black job-applicants possessed the minimum level of education that the corporation deemed necessary for those positions. The grant to the federated campaign gave the corporation three distinct benefits. It helped appease the government by demonstrating

that the corporation was doing something about the problem.
It helped strengthen an educational system that would produce more black college graduates. It provided the corporation's recruiters with a persuasive argument to convince
graduating blacks that the corporation did indeed support and
identify with the struggle to help improve the black minority's
socioeconomic lot, thereby increasing the chances that the
graduating students would want to work for the corporation.
(If the corporation plans to admit the last motive, it will have
to deduct the gift as a standard business expense, because the
IRS prohibits the use of corporate philanthropic dollars to recruit personnel.)

Motion picture companies are dependent on the legitimate theatre as a source of new talent and material. That is why it was
not surprising to learn that Columbia Pictures gave $20,000 to
twenty theatres known to be active in the production of new
plays.

The Fresh Air Fund of New York convinced Barney's clothing
store (which has a thriving children's department) to sponsor a
full-page money-solicitation ad in *The New York Times*. Barney's also donated clothes to some of the young inner-city participants who were able to take advantage of the countryside
sojourn.

Many colleges research the names of the corporations that employ a sizable number of their graduates, then approach those
firms with the persuasive argument, "Obviously, we are currently educating some of your future executives, and therefore
an investment in us is an investment for you."

Washington D.C.'s Arena Stage raised money by asking the
public to donate their gold jewelry that was lying fallow, such
as a broken watch band or the remaining half of a set of ear-
rings. Promotion costs for this "Gifts of Gold" campaign were
absorbed by the manufacturer of Old Gold cigarettes.

An inner-city high school was in need of funds to implement a
program designed to lower the drop-out rate of its students. It
was able to obtain part of the needed money and manpower

for a pilot program of automobile repair instruction from a likely funding prospect—an oil company.

The Famous Amos Chocolate Chip Cookies company donated its munchy product to Boston's Institute of Contemporary Art as a free dessert for those museumgoers who brought brown-bag lunches to attend an informal noontime gallery lecture.

Glancing down the PBS list of 1978 corporate sponsors, we observed a number of obvious match-ups, particularly in the children's programs area. General Foods, for example, sponsored "Zoom," McDonald's funded "Once Upon A Classic," and Johnson & Johnson's Baby Products supported "Mister Rogers' Neighborhood." On the local level, Chicago's PBS station was able partially to fund a Saturday rebroadcast of "The Electric Company" children's show with a grant from (you guessed it) the local electric company.

Part of the money to underwrite a cross-country tour of the "Japan Today" cultural show comprising artwork, films, and performing artists came from Matsushita Electric, the maker of Panasonic equipment.

Universities seeking doctor research fellowships for students studying toxicology would do well to approach large chemical companies, which are concerned about the potential environmental repercussions caused by their products. A case in point: Monsanto's foundation has earmarked $500,000 for such fellowships.

Who helped sponsor a Canadian theatre production on the history of the nation's fur trade? The Hudson's Bay Company is the natural answer.

In New York City there is a law that prohibits the construction of a skyscraper if it would cut off too much of the light and fresh air that would otherwise reach the sidewalk and street. If adjoining buildings are relatively low, however, their lack of height can be used in the formula that determines the maximum allowed elevation for the proposed building. Thus it is possible for nonprofit institutions that own low-rise real estate in midtown Manhattan to receive sizable dollars in exchange

for relinquishing their rights for the use of the airspace above
their property. The Museum of Modern Art was one of a number of fund-seekers that have taken advantage of this zoning
ordinance.

Equitable Life Assurance's mammoth real estate holdings in
New York City are subject to the economic health of that metropolis. This helps explain why Equitable gave $133,000 to
the nonprofit New York City Economic Development Council.

Because a number of East Indians living in greater New York
make periodic visits to their homeland, Air India willingly
gave a grant-in-aid to support an Indian music radio program.
A similar illustration: The Minneapolis Institute of Arts be-
lieved that the Scandinavian Air System was the natural air-
line to help fund its Norwegian art exhibition. The museum
was right.

The American Productivity Center in Houston, Tex. received a
quarter of a million dollars from the California-based Bank-
America Foundation. APC helps increase public awareness
about the benefits of increased productivity, a subject area that
is of obvious interest to the BankAmerica Corporation.

Clairol has a vested interest in reaching young to middle-aged
women and thus finds it advantageous to sponsor a Clairol
Loving Care Scholarship Program that helps finance tuition
costs for women wishing to return to school. The program receives good publicity and, as a bonus, its title contains the
Clairol trade name.

Syms is a New York clothing store that specializes in selling
quality-name clothing and accessories at discount prices in a
no-frills environment. How was the local PBS station able to
get Syms to be a sponsor of the "Wall Street Week" program?
Partially because the show was actively watched by many
people who worked in the Wall Street, financial district, which
is located within a short walk's distance from one of the Syms
stores.

An artist needed headlamps and accompanying electrical paraphernalia to build his "Spacescape" light sculpture exhibit in Indianapolis. A nearby General Motors facility donated the equipment a well as technical expertise.

A school for training dogs for the blind gained funds from a trust fund of Ralston Purina, a major dog-food manufacturer. The National 4-H Council received money for its youth programs because Ralston Purina is also a major breakfast-cereal maker.

Chicago's Lyric Opera raised approximately $1 million by persuading the Jim Beam distillery to make available, on an exclusive basis, a series of limited-edition decanters commemorating operatic themes. These collectors' items were sold for $200 each, or $1,600 per set.

Many wealthy people are enticed into paying the cost of a new building by the perk of having the edifice bear their name. "Tombstone philanthropy" is an apt epithet for this money-for-ego-fulfillment trade-off. A variation on this technique occurred when Lincoln Center changed the name of its previously built "Philharmonic Hall" to "Avery Fisher Hall" in return for a multimillion-dollar Fisher donation to pay for needed accoustical renovations and other expenses.

Meet with
the Corporation

You have heard the aphorism, "People give to people," a guiding light when soliciting funds from individuals. This sentiment applies equally to corporations, whose funding decisions will be made by people—the corporate officials. To perceive a corporation as a lifeless, abstract entity may be technically accurate, but that view prevents one from grasping the corporation's true nature as a vital organism whose lifeblood is the complex interaction of human beings.

When you meet with those human beings on an eyeball-to-eyeball basis, you and your organization become personalized in the executives' minds, thus adding a breath of life to your project and proposal. You also give the company officials a better opportunity to judge your character, a quality that is often hard to assess from written words.

There are also several other pivotal reasons why sitting down and talking with the company officials is usually tantamount to success: You can gather facts, gain feedback, and ask for referrals. More about those subjects later.

Setting Up the Meeting

If your previous research has not identified the correct person with whom you should meet, the quickest and usually the surest way to learn is by calling the corporation and asking to be connected "with the president's secretary." If the corporate network is enormous and involved, this person usually knows, more than the president, who has what responsibility where. One source whose information you should not automatically accept at face value is the corporate switchboard operator because more often than not, that employee is not as knowledgeable as you would hope. How many times have the operators given a grant-seeker the wrong name or even denied the existence of a contributions department?

At times, you need to schedule meetings with individuals from more than one corporate department or level. You need to take this course of action when, for instance, the local plant manager has influence but the funding decision is made at company headquarters. In such a case, meet with the grass-roots executive with the goal of securing his or her oral or written endorsement, which you can present to the top brass at the corporate command center.

Getting your foot in the executive's suite is an art form known by many, mastered by few. Your three principal methods of entry are through the influence of a mutually-known third party, by telephone, and by letter.

Setting up the Meeting: Through Third-Party Influence—By far the most effective way to open the door to an executive's office is to use the sway of one of your contacts who is on excellent terms with the executive. This is why we have emphasized in Key Six the necessity of nurturing an influential board of directors and an outside circle of supporters.

Setting Up The Meeting: By Telephone—Sometimes availing oneself of third-party influence is easier said than done. When so thwarted, use the commonplace communications instrument called the telephone. Veteran grant-seekers know that this medium is usually quicker and more effective than a letter.

Corporate executives are generally more responsive to receiving unsolicited calls than their foundation counterparts, but keep in mind that typically there is a reverse correlation between an executive's salary and his or her telephone availability. That is an unwritten business law. What you do not want to do is to forego calling the executive out of fear of being shunned. If you cannot get past the secretary's protective screen, you can at least ask that intermediary for useful facts such as verification that the executive is in fact the person to whom you should be writing for the meeting request.

When and if you are connected with the executive, speak succinctly and to the point, as is the business world's custom. Have you facts ready and your purpose clearly in mind. Tell the executive who you are, that you want to schedule a short (fifteen to thirty minutes) meeting. Briefly explain the project's goal and how it matches the corporation's objectives. Tersely emphasize your strengths and do not be reticent to mention the names of prominent people associated with your organization. Be low-keyed but enthusiastic. If the executive says yes to the meeting, quickly extend your thanks, say good-by and follow up the conversation with a confirmation letter. In that letter ask the executive to send you any material that you should read before you attend the meeting. If the company official refuses to put you on the calendar, ask the executive if you can make the request by letter and at the same time, ask what he or she would particularly like to know.

Setting Up The Meeting: By Letter—Your letter's primary purpose is to arrange a meeting, so say so up front. As with the telephone call, the letter should be brief (one page or less) but complete with the paramount information: what you want to do, how it relates with the corporation's goals, how much you are asking, and your credentials, including, if appropriate, the fact that you have tax-exempt status. Here is a sample letter:

Dear_____:

I would like to meet with you in your office for thirty minutes. My purpose is to present you the facts on how a $12,500 tax-deductible gift from your firm will enable our local library to purchase a much-needed comprehensive set of works for our new children's reading room.

I believe that your children's clothing store will want to take advantage of this unique opportunity. The books will benefit your customers and will likely provide you with favorable newspaper publicity. In addition, we are prepared to name the reading room in honor of your store.

As you are probably aware, our local library has been serving our citizenry for over 100 years and was recently selected as one of the ten best community libraries in America by the prestigious National Library Society. I am sure you know personally most of our trustees, including our chairperson and former mayor, Regina Collins.

I will call you this Friday to see if we can arrange a mutually convenient time for meeting.

Sincerely,

_____

Ideally, your organization's stationery should contain a list of your trustees and key officers. The more personal you legitimately can make the letter, the more effective it will be. A sincere "give my regards to your mother" or "hope to see you again soon at the health club" never hurts.

Using the Meeting to Gather Facts

The face-to-face encounter with the executive enables you to ask questions whose answers may not be available in the printed

literature because of oversight, recent policy changes, or a para-
noiac reluctance on the part of the company to articulate certain
guidelines in writing.

Your set of questions must be customized for each corporation
and circumstance. To give you a head start in compiling a tai-
lored set, here is a checklist of some of the queries dexterous
data-digging grant-seekers ask:

Precisely what are your objectives? What type of projects are you
seeking?

Who is my funding competition? Who else are you planning to
fund?

How much of your budget is still uncommitted?

What is your average-size grant for a project such as mine? The
minimum–maximum range?

Do you match funds?

What type of funding besides cash can you provide?

What is your preference for the style, length, and format of the
proposal?

May I examine copies of proposals for projects you have previously funded?

To whom should I submit the proposal?

How many copies do you require? If I give you extra copies, can
you circulate them in advance to your key people?

Do you have a deadline date? Would an earlier submission improve my chances? Is there a best or worst time of the year for

a submission? Should I avoid the period when your corporation is involved in the United Way drive?

Who makes the decision? When? Where?

What are your criteria? What particularly displeases your decision-makers?

When preparing the budget, what cost and accounting procedures run counter to your desires?

Would you make an on-site visit?

Do you anticipate a budgetary, policy, or any other type of change?

In what ways can I alter my project to increase its fundability?

Would you review and give your constructive criticism of my proposal as I have orally presented it to you today? Would you do the same for the final draft of my written proposal so that I can make presubmission changes?

Will you allow me to simultaneously submit two proposals slightly different in approach?

Are there any obstacles, such as legal restrictions, of which I may not be aware?

At the completion of the project, who will own the equipment? Patents? Copyrights?

Exactly what will my obligation to you be in terms of reporting? Giving you publicity?

Will I have a tightly written contract for our mutual protection?

Are you aware of other information, printed or otherwise, that I should study?

Using the Meeting to Gain Feedback

Without pushing the company official into a premature decision, try to foster (or at least be alert to) feedback on the company's satisfaction with and misgivings about various facets of your project. This insight will allow you to make critical adjustments in your written proposal by exorcising deleterious devils and spotlighting felicitous angels.

Sometimes the feedback is lucidly negative. Perhaps the corporation considers your project incompatible with their objectives or the firm will only fund your project if you make changes that are unacceptable to you. In either case, this bad news is a blessing in disguise, as it will stop you from wasting further time and money pursuing a nonexistent pot of gold

Using the Meeting to Obtain Referrals

Whenever possible, inquire during the meeting whether the executive knows of other likely funding sources for your project or organization, and whether he or she can open doors for you via a letter or telephone call. Unless you ask, you will never know whether the executive is willing and able. Do not be timid about this request; most people are flattered when asked for their advice and help.

Preparation for the Meeting

If we had a dollar for every time a grant-seeker has entered a meeting ill-prepared, we would be editing the final draft of this book on our yacht in Tahiti. Full preparation is essential because first impressions do count, and if you botch the opportunity, you may not have a second chance to sell the executive on the merits of your current and future projects.

Take your meeting preparation seriously. It should be done in such sufficient depth that you will not be caught in the embarrassing position of having asked a question whose answer is readily available in an accessible source, such as the company's published literature.

Preparation involves more than research. You must also anticipate the tough investigative questions that are the hallmark of well-trained executives. Besides, that is what these people are paid for. To prepare yourself for the barrage of barbed spears that will almost surely be flung in your direction, role-play with one or more of your colleagues using the list of questions in Part Two, starting on page 109. These role-playing sessions will help you foresee your inquisitor's probes, reveal your missing facts and murky concepts, and build your confidence.

Assemble backup material to substantiate your predications. You will need, among other documents, proof of your project's need and your qualifications.

If you plan to use slides, flip charts, or any other visual medium to help sell your project, create a tight, well-rehearsed presentation. Executives do not appreciate "home movie"-quality powwows.

Who Should Attend the Meeting?

In most cases the ideal person to attend the meeting on your behalf is one of your venerable trustees or leaders who also happens to be a close friend of the executive. However, if your illustrious representative is not thoroughly versed in your project, it is usually better to go yourself, if you are the most knowledgeable person. Or even better, both of you should go, because—as one bromide advises—two minds are better than one. And as professional negotiators know, outnumbering the other side gives your party a slight psychological advantage.

Always brief your representatives before the meeting, giving them essential data including a copy of the fact sheet we described in Key Six. Whenever your party consists of two or more people, establish a unified game plan so that each individual knows who will broach or detail which points.

Avoid overtaxing your valuable contacts. If you ask them to attend too many meetings on your behalf, you may kill their enthusiasm or even their future participation.

Tips for the Meeting

Be brief and come to the point early—you cannot afford to squander the limited number of minutes that you have been allotted to argue your case.

Conduct yourself in a professional manner but inject as much informality as the circumstances will allow. Remember, "People give to people."

Be enthusiastic—and be ready to bolster that frame of mind with hard facts.

Use trade jargon only if you are positive that everyone on the executive's side of the table understands and does not object to its use.

Do not knock your competition. When you must tell a corporation why it should support your project over another one, do it discreetly, using kid-glove allusions.

Prevarications and half-truths boomerang on the applicant when the executive ultimately detects them. If you do not know an answer, or if there are chinks in your armor, freely admit your ignorance or shortcomings.

Accentuate the positive. Rather than dwelling on what will not happen if the project goes unfunded, underscore what will happen if it is funded. And do not forget to cite your past accomplishments—executives love identifying with success.

Sell yourself, but spend much more time in telling how the project will help the corporation to meet its funding objectives.

Third-party endorsements are invaluable so long as they do not take on the aura of pressure tactics.

While most executives are civil, you will invariably encounter the maliciously petty specimen straight out of central casting. If the executive's actions or manner chafes you, bridle your swelling righteous anger. Losing one's equanimity can not only anathematize you from the corporation's future funding plans, it can create an unnecessary enemy, one that may spite you in front of his or her counterparts in other corporations.

Beware of needlessly taking on the cloak of controversy or risk. Regrettably, most executives work within a system in which the cost of failure is astronomically higher than the reward for an equivalent degree of success.

A delicate problem is what to do with the loyal donor who gives you steady streams of annual gifts. Do you dare request an increase? Or will it backfire? In the long run, you are better off asking. At the very least, request an inflation-offsetting increase.

Dress as best your pocketbook and as conservatively as your personal attire code allow. Most executives, having been conditioned in a working environment that scorns apparel nonconformity, have unconscious biases against sartorial mavericks.

Ask incisive, relevant questions (see "Using the Meeting to Gather Facts" section, on page 79).

Listen carefully for facts, opinions, and nuances.

Take notes.

If possible, end the meeting at its climax, before its pace and vitality begin to wane.

Additional Meetings

If your project is a good funding prospect for the corporation, the executive may wish to schedule one or more subsequent meetings to iron out lingering wrinkles or to gain more information. Suggest to the executive that the meeting be held on your premises, because an on-site visit will give him or her an opportunity to get acquainted with your personnel and facilities firsthand. The on-site visit also makes your project and organization more concrete in the mind of the executive, thereby improving your funding chances. A variation of the on-site visit is to send tickets to one of your performances, should the occasion present itself.

Write the Winning Proposal

The golden road to the corporate treasury is littered with the bones of fund-raisers who perished in their grant-seeking quests because, despite being armed with fundable projects, their written proposals were found wanting. Perhaps the cause was a lack of proposal-writing expertise. Perhaps it was a lack of time or care. Whatever the reason, the results are the same.

An effective proposal is imperative because it will usually be your only representative at the decision-making table. What the evaluators deduce largely will be dependent on the data printed on those pieces of paper collectively called your written proposal. If some of the information seems hazy, contradictory, incomplete, or otherwise inadequate, your proposal will be standing on weak legs because you will not be in attendance to set the record straight. Your proposal must speak for itself.

Writing Tips

No two proposals should ever be written in the same style, since each grant-seeker, proposal writer, project, and prospective donor is different. We believe, however, that the following general guidelines will be extremely helpful to the less-than-expert wordsmith.

A camel has been facetiously described as a horse designed by a committee. Do not "camelize" your proposal. Even though

many people will likely contribute ideas to it, we strongly recommend that—for the sake of cohesive style—only one person
should write the document.

Effective writing requires years of practice underpinned by in-
nate ability. If you do not have the needed writing experience
and talent, seek the volunteer or paid services of someone who
has those qualities. Exquisite style and proper grammar do
make a difference.

A bane of both novice and experienced writers is inertia. One of
the big differences between the two is that the veteran has
learned the simple yet effective remedy: Get started. Provided
that you have done your research, momentum will build with
each step you take. At this stage do not needlessly fret over
grammatical errors, absent facts, misty thinking, and other
flaws—you can rectify those problems in your second draft
once you have placed your initial thoughts on paper.

Do not wait until the last minute to write the proposal. Allow
yourself as much lead time as you can as insurance against
unforeseen obstacles. Extra time also allows you to put a draft
aside for a while, thus giving you a fresh prospective when you
retackle it a week or two later. Generally, you should start
your proposal-writing preparation two to three months prior
to submission date. Decrease or increase that estimate for less
or more complicated projects

Visualize the reader sitting across the desk from you as you write.
This mental exercise will improve the clarity of your
communication.

Humanize your project. Instead of emphasizing lifeless objects
such as buildings and equipment or abstract concepts such as
your wondrous systematic plan, stress how people will benefit
from your project.

Excite your readers with invigorating language. When fitting and
proper, use image-producing descriptions ("the overcrowded
emergency room"). The active voice ("We will train the unskilled") is always more stimulating than the passive voice
("The unskilled will be trained by us").

Anticipate as many of the reviewer's queries and objections as you possibly can. Remember, with a desk piled high with grant proposals, it is easier and less time-consuming and mind-taxing for the evaluator to look for reasons why your project should not be funded as opposed to why it should be.

Never bury your strongest selling points in the middle or at the end of your proposal, because the busy executive will probably not read your presentation in its entirety unless the opening paragraph or two grabs his or her interest. Come to the point early.

Apprise the corporation up front of the precise amount of money or type of gift-in-kind that you are requesting. The executive wants to know this bit of information at the outset.

Repetition and redundancy must be avoided, but there is nothing wrong with and much in favor of summarizing critical points.

Emphasize the significance of your project and how it dovetails with the corporation's objectives. The more you can back your arguments with statistics, the better your funding chances. When you must postulate, be sure that your assertions can be backed with at least some documentation.

Watch out for those unintended sweeping generalizations that can be found in most proposals. Be as specific as possible, employing concrete illustrations and facts.

Corporate executives respect objectivity, abhor rhetoric. Do not affront the reader's sagacity.

Overestimating an evaluator's knowledge is as bad as insulting his or her intelligence. Do not assume that the reader necessarily knows the peculiarities of your project. If you omit an essential detail, he or she may conclude that the missing element was not part of your project or, heaven forbid, that you were benighted.

At no time should your proposal be less than an honest statement of your strengths and limitations. When describing your weaknesses, however, be nonapologetic.

Short of being boastful, write in a positive, enthusiastic tone that suggests confidence.

Be brief and to-the-point, but inject warmth. A cold, impersonal style intimates much about the writer.

Keep your sentence structure simple.

Never use pseudo-erudite words such as *utilize* when *use* is shorter and has the identical meaning.

Racking your brains for the particular word that best describes a thought can be arduous at times but usually pays dividends in the long run.

Avoid jargon unless you are certain that all the proposal readers understand and welcome its use. Remember that a proposal often circulates through the corporate hallways, reaching varied specialists with dissimilar backgrounds. When in doubt, use the lay rather than the technical term.

Double-check words and phrases for possible innuendoes that may unwittingly communicate negative thoughts or erroneous conceptions.

Footnotes certainly should be used when they help remove data from the text that might otherwise slow down the reader. Overusing them, however, can create a ponderous and/or pedantic presentation.

Be aware of all restrictions, stated or implied, because once you accept the grant, you are legally bound. Moreover, if the details are spelled out in writing, you have protection in case the corporation decides to try to change the rules of the game after you have cashed the check.

Edit and rewrite your proposal once, twice, thrice ... as many times as necessary. Most people do not realize how many times the great books of the world were redrafted by their authors.

When the proposal is in its final draft stage, engage one or more third-party readers to scrutinize your developing proposal. They can help you detect blind spots resulting from your understandable zeal or lack of perspective. You may, for example, think that a fact or argument is too obvious and therefore will decide to eliminate it. Likewise, you may waste space in the proposal by elaborating on a facet that you mistakenly deemed critical.

Proposal Format

A standard proposal format for corporations does not and never will exist. Your best bet is to ask the corporation for its suggested guidelines. If these guidelines are nebulous, incomplete, or nonexistent, we have a few suggestions for you.

Proposals submitted to corporations are generally much shorter and less formalized than those proffered to foundations and governmental agencies.

Proposal length can vary from a half-page to scores of pages, depending on the complexity of your project and the desires of the corporation. When in doubt, use the "shorter the better" rule of thumb, because that coincides with the wishes of most corporate funding officers.

If the proposal is brief, present it in a letter format, one or two pages long. More-involved proposals will entail a many-paged document, fronted and backed by, respectively, a cover letter and addendum, two elements discussed farther along.

Letters are almost always single-spaced; document-style proposals should normally be double-spaced to enhance reading ease. Also, for the sake of the reader's eye, the proposal should be amply endowed with wide margins and other white-space-preserving devices. Another technique for improving readability and visual appeal is the adept use of headings and subheadings.

Yes, executives do judge a proposal—at least to some degree—on its cover and general appearance. We therefore advise using quality materials—but not too exquisite, lest the executive think you profligate.

A rag bond paper with at least a 20-pound weight classification provides durability. Its thickness tactually suggests substance.

Let neatness be one of your precepts. Your final draft should be typed by a professional secretary, one who does not blemish the pages with White-out and erasure marks.

Your proposal, irrespective of its length, should logically flow in the following order:

NEED

↓

OBJECTIVE

↓

METHODS

The need fashions your objective, which in turn determines your methods, which in turn mold yet another component of your proposal, the budget.

The other four standard components of the body of a proposal are a concise introduction and summary, your qualifications, a description of how you plan to measure and evaluate the success of your project, and—if applicable—your project's future.

The standard sequence for the eight proposal-components is:

I. Introduction and Summary
II. The Need
III. The Objective
IV. The Methods
V. Our Qualifications
VI. The Evaluation
VII. The Budget
VIII. The Program's Future

We have phrased these eight headings in the traditional mode, which should probably be used whenever you are writing for a conservative-minded evaluator. However, if you can pre-determine that the evaluator will not look askance on your using evocative phraseology, we strongly suggest that you employ ac-tion headlines. To illustrate: Substitute "Objective: Curing Insomnia" for the strictly abstract headline, "Objective." If used proficiently and in the right situation, this tactic creates an aura of excitement and impending accomplishment.

Title Page

Here is the title-page layout that we have found to be very effective:

A proposal for a
$50,000 GRANT

To establish
A DAY CARE CENTER IN BELL ACRES

Submitted to
THE XYZ CORPORATION

on
May 10, 1980

by
Your name
Your title
YOUR ORGANIZATION
Your address
Your telephone number

As you can see, the magnitude of the request will be quickly and unequivocally grasped by the executive. The same is true for the project's purpose.

"Introduction and Summary" Section

Though this is your proposal's first narrative section, we advise you—for the sake of perspective—to write it after you have drafted the ensuing seven sections, from "The Need" through "The Program's Future."

If properly scribed, your "Introduction and Summary" section will enable the executive to know immediately whether your project correlates with the corporation's funding goals. If it does not, the executive saves valuable time by not having to read farther. If it appears that your project is a match-up, then the executive can study your proposal's individual sections with increased vigor and insight.

Briefly state your request (in a little more detail than you did in the title page), then succinctly describe your project's need, significance, and beneficiaries and—perhaps most important of all—how your project relates to the prospective donor's goals.

The "Need" Section

A common form of "granticide" is assuming that all the people who will be reading your proposal share your awareness of the need. Almost surely there will be lurking within the corporate fortress at least one key official afflicted with ignorance or blind spots.

It is incumbent on you to sharply define the need in terms of its urgency, magnitude, and parameter.

Your predications must be quantified with hard statistics (specifying, for instance, the number, socioeconomic status, and geographical scope of your beneficiaries). Authoritative third-party verification must be presented, too. Serious-minded evaluators also want to know who else is trying to solve the need and in what ways.

The "Objective" Section

Do not confuse "objective" with "methods," as do most proposal writers. Your objective is what you want to accomplish, whereas your methods are the means of accomplishing your objective. To illustrate our point, consider the sentence, "Our objective is to set up remedial reading programs for high school drop-outs." That is a method rather than an objective; ". . . to improve the reading skills . . ." is the objective.

Your objective must satisfy the following three criteria. First, it must be attainable (do you really have the time, abilities, and resources to conduct the remedial reading program?). Second, it must be practical (assigning a full-time Ph.D. for each remedial reading student is attainable but not practical—there are better uses for a Ph.D.'s expertise). Third, your objective must be measurable in quantitative terms (you could specify, for instance, anticipated percentile increases in reading speed).

Finally, within this section you should try to point out that your project's objective matches that of the corporation.

The "Methods" Section

For every objective there is an array of possible methods for achieving it. What the evaluator wants to know is whether you have selected the best set of methods. To convince him or her of this fact, you need to demonstrate that you are aware of the pluses and minuses of the various options and that you know how to deal with potential pitfalls and bottlenecks.

Many corporate executives believe—with some justification—that most nonprofit organizations are poorly managed. One way to overcome this bias is to impress the corporation with your businesslike approach to planning your operations. To help you do this, present your methods in a step-by-step timetable format that will enable the readers to grasp at a glance your priorities and time frames.

"Our Qualifications" Section

You may know how good you are but do the evaluators? You must convince them not only that you are qualified but also that you are the most qualified individual or organization available. Incorporate into this section your organization's credentials and biographical sketches of key staff members. Highlight your unique selling proposition (discussed in Key Five, page 50). Also list the names, addresses, and telephone numbers of impartial individuals who are in a position to verify your qualifications (secure permission first).

The "Evaluation" Section

An alarming number of corporations in the distant and recent pasts have not attempted to have the results of their philanthropic dollars measured and evaluated. Nowadays this outrage is abating, as more and more corporations are demanding that if a nonprofit organization is to receive corporate contributions, then that organization is going to have to have a program to tally and analyze the effect of the gift.

A sound evaluation program uses objective rather than subjective criteria—ones that can be quantified. One illustration is, "Our goal is to increase attendance by 20 percent." If the results of your project cannot be measured in quantitative terms, your chances of obtaining a grant are low.

For credibility's sake, it is a good idea to have a third party (the more distinguished, the better) to design and execute your evaluation program. Your cost for this outside service should be included in your budget.

The "Budget" Section

The size of the budget will reflect your methods. When estimating a budget, be as realistic as possible. If you underestimate your budget in the belief that it will make your project more appealing to the corporation, you are surely mistaken, since the evaluators probably will question your administrative competence. If you go to the other extreme by padding your budget, your subterfuge likely will be detected because most evaluators are well-tutored in the analysis of financial documents.

Keep your budget presentation brief—one to two single-spaced typewritten pages will be more than adequate for virtually all projects. Use the allotted area frugally, as you must inject into it ample detail. Being specific is particularly important for categories and subcategories such as salaries, consulting fees, and travel expenses—items that have a natural propensity for raising the eyebrows of Doubting Thomas executives.

Funds that have already been donated or firmly committed to the project should be brought quickly to the reader's attention. One established method of indicating these guaranteed contributions is by placing a footnoted asterisk after the appropriate dollar figures as we did in our sample proposal in Part Three, pages 124 and 125.

Whether your budgeting period has a one-month or a multiyear life span, be sure it affords you sufficient time. Many neophyte grant-seekers underestimate the time it will take to complete a project and therefore are saddled with having to pay out of their own pockets postbudgetary overruns such as salaries and rent.

Finally, double-check, if not triple-check, for arithmetic errors, those culprits that seem to sneak into proposals in the middle of the night while you sleep.

If neither you nor the corporation have a preferred budget format, use our suggested nine-category outline:

> Personnel
> Outside Services
> Rent
> Utilities
> Equipment

Supplies
Travel and Meetings
Miscellaneous Expenses
General Reserve

Adjust the categories to your circumstances. If your subcategory for medicine is relatively large, give it its own category. Likewise, if your budget calls for scant or nil equipment purchases, eliminate that category and itemize the equipment, if any, within your "Miscellaneous Expense" category. Now, for some of the finer points:

Personnel—This one category will probably consume at least half of your operating budget. The more your project is service-oriented in nature, the bigger the share will be. In most cases you should break down this category into two subcategories: "Salary and Wages" and "Fringe Benefits." Your fringe-benefits components (unemployment insurance, private retirement contributions, etc.) can be itemized individually or can be expressed as a percentage (about 10 to 20 percent) of the payroll—ask the corporation for its preference. When specifying the personnel costs for multiyear budgets, be sure to take into account inflation-based and merit raises.

Outside Services—Legal, accounting, public relations, and consulting in general are among the outside professional services listed in this budget category. In addition to the services you will purchase, list any donated services along with their estimated value—but only if you are positive that the promised volunteered assistance will be forthcoming.

Rent—If you anticipate that the evaluators may view your rent as excessive, prepare to justify that abnormality by, for example, obtaining a letter from a local real-estate board verifying that rents in your area are higher than the citywide norm.

Utilities—Telephone, telegraph, teletype, and—if not included the rent—gas, water, and electricity fall within this category. Should your message units and/or long-distance charges be exceptionally high, give sufficient detail and explanation.

Equipment—If an item has a minimum value of, say, $100 or $200, and if you expected to use it for longer than a year, then list it in the "Equipment" rather than the "Supplies" category. Examples of this type of asset include office furnishings (desks, chairs, files, cabinets, curtains, carpets) and office equipment (typewriters, tape recorders, photocopy machines, calculators, postage meters). The equipment does not necessarily have to be purchased, since it can also be rented, leased, donated, or borrowed. To eliminate postproject disputes, be sure to specify in your proposal who will own and take possession of the equipment at the termination of the project.

Supplies—If you plan to spend a relatively large sum for a particular item (printed stationery or postage stamps, for instance), feature that item in its own budget subcategory. Items of less expense can be grouped collectively in a "General Office Expense" subcategory.

Travel and Meetings—Evaluators are especially suspicious about expenses for out-of-town travel. Do not amass your costs under a single umbrella such as "a trip to Bangor, Maine" if the total exceeds approximately $100. Rather, individually itemize the larger expense items such as transportation, hotel, and seminar fees.

Miscellaneous Expenses—This is a catch-all category for small expenses that cannot be pigeonholed into the other budget categories.

General Reserve—No matter how tightly you plan your budget, unexpected expenditures loom on the horizon. Some corporations will allow you to include a reserve for those contingencies (ask them), provided that the figure does not exceed approximately 5 percent of your total budget. If it does, the corporate executive will rightly conclude that you did not adequately dissect your budget.

"The Program's Future" Section

Incorporate this section only if your project will extend beyond the funding period of your requested grant. In order to allay the corporation's fear that its good money may sluice down the drain, you must present a realistic plan on how you will keep the project afloat financially after you have expended the corporation's dollars or gifts-in-kind.

Your Proposal's Addendum

Use an addendum wisely. It is meant to be the receptacle for supporting data too ponderous or ancillary to be placed in the body of your proposal but too significant to be omitted. This material could include letters of endorsement or certificates, personnel vitae, statistical tables, publicity clippings, and your annual report. Keep your addendum as small as possible. If it must be large, place it in a separate binder and be sure to label each subunit of the addendum clearly.

Your Cover Letter

If your proposal is document- as opposed to letter-style, you will need to prepare a cover letter to give the evaluator a quick overview of the nature and size of your request, your credentials, and how your request relates with the corporation's objectives. The heart of your letter will be a condensation of the already condensed descriptions contained in the "Introduction and Summary" section of your proposal. Your letter should also convey enthusiasm and a willingness to supply the corporation with any additional information it may require.

Compose your cover letter after you have completed the first draft of your proposal and addendum. Give this task your diligent attention, because your cover letter is the first piece of paper the evaluator will see—and first impressions have been known to bend the judgment of more than a few evaluators.

SAMPLE COVER LETTER

Dear [Corporate Executive]:

I am pleased to submit to your company, Acme Industries, our proposal requesting a grant of $9,000 to pay our out-of-pocket costs for a two-month summer basketball league for high school students living in the economically depressed XYZ neighborhood.

We estimate that 200 of your workers' children will be participating in our proposed project. Moreover, the league will also benefit 1,000 other high school students, a group that obviously contains many of your future employees.

The proposed league is enthusiastically supported by Mayor Timothy Jones and School Superintendent Nancy Wong, among others. Our organization, as you may know, has the needed credentials. For instance, we have been conducting high school summer-sports camp programs with success over the past several years.

I cannot thank you enough for having given me the opportunity to discuss this project with you in our previous meetings. Please let me know if you want any additional information.

Sincerely,

Always be brief—you will need at the most a single page. Use your official letterhead; if it lists the names of your board of directors and key officers, all the better. Try to personalize the letter by referring to matters such as previous meetings. For sake of consistency, the letter's signatory and date should be identical with those on the proposal's title page.

Submitting Your Proposal

Business protocol virtually necessitates that you submit the original typed copy of your proposal. If the corporation requests additional copies, these usually can be photocopied rather than typed individually.

Before sliding the proposal into the envelope, scrutinize your masterpiece for possible damaging secretarial or clerical blunders, such as misspellings, typos, and missing material. Be sure the envelope is strong, sturdy, and protective, because unless you deliver the proposal by hand, the package will likely undergo mishandling, mangling, and dog-earring in the process.

Deliver the proposal early enough to give yourself a safe margin ahead of the deadline date. Whenever convenient and possible, add a personal touch by delivering the proposal from your hand into the executive's hand. Delivery by messenger is usually your next-best bet, although the U.S. Post Office medium can suffice, too. If you use the postal service, we suggest you send your proposal by certified mail with a "return receipt request," which is, for your purpose, just as effective and less costly than registered mail.

Normally you will be making multisubmissions, sending a customized version of your basic proposal to two or more funding sources. In order to be a successful grant-seeker, simultaneous submission is practically essential. There is nothing improper about this strategy so long as you apprise each prospective donor of your deed.

While you are in the act of submitting your proposal circulate an extra copy or two around to people connected with your organization. A proposal, if well-conceived and executed, can be an informative internal-communications tool.

Follow Through

You have just returned from lunch and there, sitting on your desk, is an unopened letter waiting to reveal to you the corporation's decision and, if it is a favorable one, perhaps an enclosed check. Consumed with curiosity, you rip open the envelope and read the tidings. From that moment on, whether you kiss the letter or crumple it in despair, you still have much grant-seeking-related work to do if you want to sustain and enhance your fund-raising efforts in the future. You must follow through.

If the Answer Is "Yes"

Before the sun sets, mail a thank-you letter written in a personal tone befitting your gratitude. A brief restatement of what you plan to do with the money and how you intend to keep the corporation abreast of your program reassures the executive, as does your acknowledgment of (if appropriate) your receipt of the check.

You will also want to notify the various people inside and outside of your organization who will be affected by the grant. An announcement of the gift in the press usually provides image-building publicity for you and the corporation, so explore this opportunity with the executive. Perhaps the corporation can have its own PR department or agency place the story if you are insufficiently staffed in this discipline. Should you decide to release the news yourself, check first with the corporation for its approval.

Once in a blue moon a multiple-submitted proposal will be accepted by more than one corporation. Should this rare fortuitous fate befall you, analyze the broad net effect of accepting or rejecting each offer, then choose accordingly. For the sake of the future, broach your "thanks, but no thank you" declination to your surplus corporate givers with utmost diplomacy. And who knows—you may be able to convince those corporations to use the money to fund one of your other projects.

If the Answer Is "No"

People who shy away from situations in which they may be rebuffed should not be grants persons. Being told no is an occupational hazard that must be accepted as part of the normal routine. Unless you are extremely lucky (and few of us are), the odds against even one of your best-bet corporations funding your project are high, perhaps ten to one. What counts more is not how many times your proposals are rejected, but the number of instances in which they are accepted. Imagine this scene: You are in your rubber boots standing knee-deep in a cool running mountain brook. You probably will not catch a trout for your frying pan unless you are prepared to cast your fly numerous times unsuccessfully.

Uncrumple that reject letter and compose a thank-you note on this order:

Dear [Corporate Executive]:

We appreciate your having taken the time to review our proposal.

We are obviously disheartened that you could not fund our PQR project, because senior citizens in our community are in dire need of the medical services. At the same time, we recognize that it would be impossible for you to fulfill every request, as the demand for your contribution dollars exceeds the supply.

I would like very much to keep in touch with you. Perhaps one of our next projects will better match the philanthropic objectives of your corporation.

Sincerely,

Your goodwill-building thank-you missive will probably make, as movie critics love to pen, a "powerful and gripping" impression on the mind of the executive, because few grant-seekers send them.

Another seldom-initiated yet vital postreject task is to attempt to ascertain why your proposal went unfunded. If you can discern the reasons, you may be able to improve that proposal or any of your future written funding requests. One frequently overlooked source for the analytical impact is the corporation—that is, if the executive is willing to be candid. Too many corporate-funding officers hide behind subterfuges such as "sorry, our budget was already committed" rather than risk crushing your ego or raising your hackles by telling you the real reasons why your proposal was put to the sword. Because some corporate executives do not wish to disclose their true motives, you must not automatically accept a postmortem report at face value.

Compared with their foundation and governmental-agency funding counterparts, corporations tend to be much more willing to negotiate a rejected proposal. If you think you have located the proposal's impediments and can rectify them, ask the executive if he or she would be willing to sit down with you to restructure the proposal so that it becomes mutually agreeable.

Another possibility is to raise part of the requested funds from another source, then go back to the corporation saying, "We now need only half of what we originally asked because another firm has committed to us the other portion." This appeal sometimes compels the executive to take a second look at your proposal.

If Word Is Slow in Coming

Most but not all corporate executives will, out of courtesy, promptly acknowledge the receipt of your proposal and/or inform you if the decision will take longer than normally expected. Other executives are more derelict. Unless you give these officers a gentle nudge, your proposal may gather dust on a credenza or suffer similar misfortune. If you have not heard any word from the corporation within two or three weeks after you submit your proposal, by all means make a friendly query by telephone or letter.

Reporting Progress

By creating and carrying out a sound reporting and record-keeping procedure, you can only impress a business executive. This practice is becoming all the more important as more corporations are realizing that they should measure the results of their contribution dollars.

Prepare for the corporation a detailed final report that includes the results of the evaluation system that you described in your proposal (see Key Nine, page 96). If the project is long, also submit brief interim reports (perhaps every three months) summarizing your progress, plus a brief description of any stumbling blocks you are encountering and how you plan to step over or around them. A supplement or alternative to interim reports is to invite the executive to visit your project in midstream.

Think Long-term

Picking the fruit off the corporate money tree next year will be much easier if you take the time and foresight to do a little cultivating today. It is a profitable and proven investment.

First, keep your best prospects informed about and as involved with your organization as possible. Pay particular attention to your current givers, as they are probably your most likely sources for your next round of funding. At the same time, do not assume anything. Just because a corporation has been giving money to you for the last ten years is no guarantee that you will receive even a penny next year. A change in leadership at the corporation could, for instance, curtail the funding because the new chief executive does not identify with your project.

Also, continue to reassess the funding possibilities of your nongivers, including those corporations that financially supported you once a few years back. Time brings changes in personnel and policy.

Constantly update your grant-seeking records. When there is an announcement in the newspaper of a change in key executives at one of your best-bet corporations, make note of it while the fact is still fresh in your memory.

Get publicity for yourself. This vehicle keeps your name in the minds of the corporations up and beyond means normally available to you.

If a corporation gives you less than you anticipated, do not grumble, at least not within earshot of the donor. Even a $1 gift keeps the door ajar for future funding.

Do not look upon the corporate executive just as the dispenser of funds. He or she may be able to contribute some sound ideas on how to implement your project. If this becomes the case, you gain an added benefit: The corporate executive will have become more involved in your organization and thus will become a better friend in court when your next proposal is evaluated.

Sometimes the concept for a project emanates from within the corporation, which then scouts around for a nonprofit organization to put the plan into action. Get the inside track to those windfalls by from time to time asking the corporation if it has any germinating ideas that you may be able to execute.

PART TWO

Questions Evaluators Ask

The methods corporations use to evaluate proposals are as varied as the corporations themselves. We have found that even within the same corporation there are evaluation discrepancies because even though two corporate decision-makers may use the same printed official criteria, each brings into the equation his or her own set of biases and misconceptions.

Still, there are certain basic questions that most evaluators ask themselves. These queries are worth studying because they can help you discover and strengthen the soft underbelly of your written proposal or oral presentation before it is pierced by the evaluator's probing stiletto.

Is There a Need for the Project?

What is the project's need? Significance? Urgency? Are all predications documented?

Who will benefit from the project? Is the project a priority for the beneficiaries? What are the populations, geographics, socio-economics, and other demographics of the intended beneficiaries?

How does the project relate to the bigger picture? [For instance, if you plan to research how electrical particles can be used in the treatment of cancer, the evaluator will want to know how your tile fits into the general cancer-research mosaic.]

Does the project duplicate or overlap the past, present or planned projects of other individuals or organizations?

Is the Project Relevant to Us?

Was the proposal properly submitted in terms of our required or desired format and deadline?

Does the project mesh with our corporate-giving guidelines in terms of objective? Field of interest? Type of funding (cash or gifts-in-kind)? Size of gift? Grant period? Geographic scope?

Does the request fit within our minimum–maximum funding bracket? [If the answer is no, chances are you did not do your homework before submitting your proposal.]

Is the project the best investment for our philanthropic dollars? How does the project compare with the other funding requests we are evaluating in terms of our priorities?

Will funding this project concentrate too much of our philanthropic dollars in one area?

Are we the best, most logical funding source, or should it be funded in part or totally by governmental agencies, independent foundations, federated funding agencies, community service organizations, individual donors, or even another corporation?

Would we get more PR mileage by being the sole supporter?

Would a matching fund arrangement give us more impact leverage? Will our donation encourage other donors to jump on the bandwagon?

Even though our goal is not to make a profit from our contribution, would the donation benefit us in the long term by, say, providing us with a new technology that emanated out of a funded research project? Is this profit potential so obvious that we should be funding out of our business-expense rather than philanthropic budget?

How many people will learn of our gift? [Many corporations would prefer to support a large-audience dance company of mediocre repute than a small, experimental, highly acclaimed one performing before small audiences. Sometimes, however, a corporation is willing to trade quantity for quality of audience in order to reach opinion-makers, so long as the quantitative sacrifice is kept within bounds.]

What are the benefits to our various publics, including governmental bodies, the media, trade unions, trade organizations and most particularly, employees, stockholders, and customers? How will those publics react if we do make the donation?

Will the project backfire on us because of being hit by a lawsuit? Receiving unfavorable publicity? Being "double-crossed?" [An illustration would be a theatre group staging an antinuclear skit with the money it received from a power company.]

Is the Applicant Qualified?

What is the track record of the individual or organization?

Is the applicant financially stable? Is there a chance of financial collapse before the completion of the project?

Who else is supporting the organization? Why? To what degree?

Does the applicant possess or have access to the needed facilities and equipment? If some services and equipment are to be donated, what are the chances of their not being delivered as promised?

What is the quality of management? [Corporations want to know that the recipient is capable of running a tight administrative ship—after all, the corporation expects the same of itself.]

Are personnel assignments clear and explicit? Is each individual qualified?

Do the key people have the necessary enthusiasm and personal character? Do they fully understand the value and scope of the project? Will each individual perform the work promised or are some of them merely lending the project their illustrious name or titles as window dressing? [A not-uncommon example of this artifice is for a research project grant-seeker to embellish the personnel roster with the name of a prominent Nobel laureate professor whose role, in fact, will be largely titular.]

How involved, influential, and qualified are the applicant's board of directors or trustees? Are their functions merely ceremonial?

If outside consultants and subcontractors are used, are they qualified and are their charges and fees reasonable?

Does the project have the full support and cooperation of the applicant's entire organization?

Is the project a priority for the applicant?

Does the applicant have sufficient reputation and contacts outside the organization to accomplish its mission?

Does the applicant have the necessary authority (rights to a patent, for instance), legal status (tax-exemption, if it be required) and professional credentials?

Has the applicant furnished the names of people who can help verify the applicant's qualifications (and assertions in general)?

Is someone else better qualified to undertake the project?

Are the Methods Practical?

Does the proposal specify who will do what, with, or to whom—and why, when, and where? Are those methods realistic? Cost-effective?

Is the budget sufficiently detailed? Are the cost estimates realistic? Is the budget size consistent with the applicant's budgetary patterns, or is the applicant attempting to expand too quickly?

Are the methods in keeping with the applicant's character and by-laws? With governmental regulations?

What are the chances of success?

Is the applicant cognizant of potential pitfalls?

Is the applicant aware of the other possible options for accomplishing the objective? Is the applicant current on what others in the field are doing?

Are the Results Measurable?

Can the success be measured and evaluated? By whom? How? When? To what degree of accuracy?

What Are the Long-term Implications?

Will the project have a positive, far-reaching impact beyond itself? [To illustrate, a dance program sponsored on PBS may help small dance companies throughout the land because the televised performance will probably stimulate public interest in dance, which in turn increases ticket sales, which in turn financially strengthens these local cultural ensembles.]

If the project fails, will it impair the opportunity or ability of another organization tackling the same problem?

Will the applicant become chronically dependent on our beneficence? Once having given our first-round support, will community pressure force us to keep the applicant afloat?

Less-than-responsible Criteria

The questions in the preceding sections are the ones asked by honorable corporate philanthropists. Their less-than-responsible colleagues sometimes bypass or supplement those questions with absurd or ulterior-motivated considerations along these lines:

It's my alma mater.

I may get my picture in the newspaper.

If my company becomes a sponsor, I get to meet some famous sports stars.

I have so much fun at their annual charity masquerade ball.

My daughter had her appendix removed in that hospital.

Johnny, its executive director, is the nice guy with whom I periodically play golf. [The corollary of this rationale is, "I do not like that organization's treasurer."]

It's only a hundred dollars. [If this justification is used often enough, the aggregate size of the gifts can be sizable.]

How can we not give to that charity if everyone else has?

Wouldn't it be quicker and easier to repeat last year's gifts?

If the charity got along without our money last year, why can't it get along without us this year?

It is asking for $24,000 and that is exactly the amount in our budget that we must donate before Friday's deadline.

We received this proposal first. [The first-come-first-serve mentality.]

The organization is well known. [The fame of an applicant is more important to some contributors than the quality of the project.]

I love opera.

I am being creative by funding our city's best-known art museum. [Some local cultural units are so staid in outlook that they could hardly be called creative.]

It's my mother-in-law's pet charity.

Our president serves on their board.

My chairperson is on my back.

How do you say no to the United Way?

Mary helped my charity last month, and now I will return the favor by supporting the one she is chairing.

The project is nonestablishment. [An executive of a major tobacco firm once said, "Corporations usually do not like to get involved with avant-garde projects, so they avoid anything that's controversial."]

While we do not know whether the project will do much good to the community, we do know that it will not do us any harm.

I do not want to rock the boat.

If the project backfires, I may lose standing within my corporation and therefore may jeopardize my promotions, my pay raises, and perhaps even my job security. [A corporate executive has a family to support and a mortgage to pay and like most people, is concerned about being canned.]

I do not have time to read any more proposals.

PART THREE

Sample Proposal

The project depicted in our sample proposal is fictitious, as are the statistics, people, and organizations listed. We have two reasons for electing to write a proposal from scratch rather than succumbing to the temptation of simply reprinting one of the many funded-proposals ensconced in our file cabinets. First, the subject matter of actual proposals are too narrowly focused to be good instructional vehicles by themselves for any person not in the same field. Our Music-in-the-Street project will relate (at least on a personal level) with nearly all our readers, and therefore, we believe it will be more useful than, say, a proposal for a grant to research how subatomic-particle radiation affects cellular structures. Our second reason is that our created proposal better enables us to illustrate a greater variety of proposal-writing principles.

A proposal for a
$18,849 grant

To initiate
A SUMMER MUSIC-IN-THE-STREETS PROGRAM
TO HELP ASPIRING MUSICIANS

Submitted to
WXXX BROADCASTING CORPORATION

on
April 30, 1980

by
Coretta Martin
Executive Director
METROPOLIS MUSIC SOCIETY, INC.
502 Essex Avenue
Metropolis, USA 90008
(820) 666-1221

Introduction and Summary

This is a request to **WXXX** Broadcasting Corporation from our organization, the nonprofit Metropolis Music Society, for a three-month grant of $18,849. This money will permit us to initiate a new and exciting summer Music-In-The-Streets (MITS) program for our city.

Our MITS project will help improve the proficiency of aspiring musicians. This will be accomplished by providing the musicians with the unique opportunity of being able to earn their lesson and basic-living expenses by and while performing for pedestrians on midtown sidewalks, with the blessing of the City Council.

We are submitting this proposal to **WXXX** because your radio station is the city's most public-service-minded broadcaster of music. Moreoever, we know that **WXXX** has often expressed its strong desire to help further the careers of promising musicians, whatever their musical pursuits.

Although the overall MITS budget is $23,499, we need only $18,849 from **WXXX**, because our organization is able to donate $4,650 in facilities and services.

As our other success stories will help verify, the Metropolis Music Society is qualified to conduct the MITS project.

The Need

Eminent musicologist Dr. James Flanagan noted in the February 1980 article in the highly respected *Music and Culture Quarterly* that the careers of many aspiring musicians are "tragically nipped in the bud." In order to pay their basic living expenses, the artists have to resort to unrelated employment, thereby sapping the time and energy available for their practice. Dr. Flanagan further emphasized that the fund shortage usually places lessons beyond their reach. In an editorial in the same issue, the journal's publisher wrote, "If a musician is to develop virtuosity, he or she must play in front of people rather than alone in a practice room."

According to the director of the Cultural Affairs Department, Roberta Clark, our city has approximately 5,000 musicians representing various styles—from folk to classical music—who fit Dr. Flanagan's description. Yet, there is currently no effective local program to help them increase their income, practice time, lessons, and opportunities to perform in front of live audiences.

The Objective

Metropolis Music Society wishes to implement a three-month summer MITS project. Its objective is to create and manage a program that will allow aspiring musicians to increase the money they earn so that they can better pursue their career goals. The secondary objective is to give these musicians a chance to perform in front of people.

We believe our project correlates with one of your objectives. Last month, for instance, your Executive Vice-President, James Dean, stated in one of your editorials, "WXXX is in favor of subsidizing promising musicians who wish to further their training." Furthermore, by sponsoring MITS you will win the invaluable goodwill of the public and your listeners, because WXXX will be helping to create a more pleasant environment for the people of our city. Your promotion people will have a splendid opportunity to develop a creative campaign built around your sponsorship.

The Methods

We recognize that there are four essentials for a workable MITS program. First, the city must pass an ordinance making it legal for MITS-sanctioned musicians to perform for donations along the midtown sidewalks (we have already managed to have the ordinance passed[1]). Second, MITS must select qualified participants. Third, MITS must administer and coordinate the as-

---

[1] See Addendum for documentation.

signments of safe, productive, and specific sidewalk locations and schedules. Fourth, the public must be made aware of the program so that it will be encouraged to toss coins into the participating musicians' money boxes emblazoned with the official MITS seal of approval.

JUNE (*First Half*)—Hire the staff: project director and administrative assistant/secretary. Set up the office (install telephones, purchase stationery, etc). Retain the Baker & Rodriguez Public Relations Agency to develop a well-conceived publicity program. Identify the best locations and time periods for the sidewalk performances. Create a scheduling system. Purchase a $1,000,000 public liability and damage insurance policy to cover the MITS participants while they perform in the streets. Sign up one dozen musicians to be the first participants (we already have their names and commitments). This limited-scale operation will help debug the program before starting the publicity campaign.

JUNE (*Second Half*)—The Baker & Rodriguez Agency will contact the media. It will place a particular emphasis on getting the local TV stations to cover the story, using as subjects MITS's original dozen participants. The MITS Participants Selection Committee will audition an estimated 500 applicants to select approximately 100 talented new participants representing a cross-section of different music styles and instruments.

JULY—The program will be in full operation. Besides performing their normal administrative chores, the staff will research, analyze, and implement new ways to improve the MITS program.

AUGUST—The program's success will be evaluated. The results will be incorporated into the program director's final report to be written during the last week of August. On August 31, the project will be put into limbo until the following summer.

Our Qualifications

Metropolis Music Society is a tax-exempt 501 (C) 3 nonprofit organization[2] founded in 1954. We currently have 1,524 paid-in-full ($20 per year) members and a board of trustees comprising some of the key cultural leaders of our city.[2]

Our chartered purpose is to help aspiring musicians, irrespective of race, creed, or sex. Some of our successful projects include the weekly Chamber Music Showcase at the Swallow Hill Library, the annual T. R. Jones Seminar that gives constructive advice to graduating high school students who are considering a career in music, and the publishing of the *Monthly Note,* a newsletter for local music teachers.

Our project director will be Gladys Mittner, former Associate Director of the TransAmerican Symphony Orchestra. She also created and administered the city school system's "Musical Interludes," a junior high-school assembly program featuring local musicians. See the Addendum for her vitae.

The Participants Selection Committee will comprise five prominent local citizens of diverse musical backgrounds. These volunteers are nightclub owner Benita Louzeiro, classical-music teacher Sophie Bukowski, music-store proprietor Alexander Fabian, musical-theatre impresario Heidi Utzinger, and retired opera singer Serge Rogoff. See the Addendum for brief biographical sketches.

The Evaluation

Our goal is to generate an average of 500 performance hours per midweek day once our project is in full swing. (That number extrapolates to approximately 10,000 hours per month, which, we estimate, would put at least $60,000 per month in much-needed money into the pockets of our 100 participants.) The

---

[2] See Addendum for documentation.

Stenhouse Market Research Company will impartially estimate the average daily hours by having members of its staff survey the midtown streets on three randomly selected, midweek days during the first two weeks of August. The exact days will be unknown to us until after the survey has been completed.

Budget

Note: MITS will operate during its first year for only three months, from June 1 through August 31, 1980, the period covered by this budget. The facilities and services that will be donated by our organization are indicated with asterisks.

		TOTALS
PERSONNEL:		
Executive Director = $2,000 per month	$6,000	
Administrative assistant/secretary = $1,000 per month	$3,000	
Fringe benefits = 10% of total salaries	$900	
SUBTOTAL: PERSONNEL		$9,900
OUTSIDE SERVICES:		
Legal services = $200 per month	$600	
Bookkeeping = $100 per month	$300	
PR consulting services = $1,250 per month	$3,750	
Program-evaluation service	$650	
SUBTOTAL: OUTSIDE SERVICES		$5,300
RENT:		
500 square feet of furnished office space = $1,000 per month		$3,000*
UTILITIES:		
Telephone installation charge	$30	
Telephone service = $25 per month	$75	
Local telephone message units, 300 per month = 10¢	$90	
Gas and electric (part of rent)	$0	
SUBTOTAL: UTILITIES		$195
EQUIPMENT:		
Rental of typewriter and calculator = $50 per month	$150*	
Purchase of portable public address microphone (owership will belong to WXXX)	$250	
SUBTOTAL: EQUIPMENT		$400

SUPPLIES:
Stationery	$250	
Printed literature	$500	
Seal of approval decals	$200	
Postage stamps	$100	
General office expenses	$200	
SUBTOTAL: SUPPLIES		$1,250

TRAVEL AND MEETINGS:
Local transportation (taxi, bus, etc.) @ $50 per month	$150	
Executive director's one-day trip to Megacity to share information with a similar project being started in that municipality: $95 for round-trip train ticket, $50 for one night's lodging, and $50 per diem expense	$195	
SUBTOTAL: TRAVEL AND MEETINGS		$345

MISCELLANEOUS EXPENSES:
Public liability and damage insurance	$490	
Assigned overhead (this is the portion of Metropolis Music Society's overhead that is allocated to the MITS operating budget for miscellaneous services rendered as itemized in this proposal's addendum)	$1,500*	
SUBTOTAL: MISCELLANEOUS EXPENSES		$1,990

GENERAL RESERVE FOR CONTINGENCIES:
@ 5% of the overall itemized budget	$1,119

GRAND TOTAL:
TOTAL BUDGET	$23,499
LESS DONATED FACILITIES AND SERVICES	$4,650*
FUNDS STILL NEEDED	$18,849

The Program's Future

The City's Cultural Affairs Department has agreed in writing[3] to absorb the entire operational costs of the program in the ensuing years if we can attain a daily average of 500 performance hours for Monday through Friday.

[3] See Addendum for documentation.

According to Baker & Rodriguez, MITS will likely gain national publicity via network news shows and news magazines. That exposure will encourage other organizations in other cities to establish similar programs.

PART FOUR

Information

Sources

About Strictly Foundation-Oriented Sources

For the reasons we have explained above, we have limited the focus of this book to raising funds from corporations rather than from foundations, a vast field unto itself. Consequently, we have not given in Part Four individual entries to information sources that deal with foundation grant-seeking unless they happen to cover, to a reasonable degree, the topic of corporate grant-seeking as well. *The Art of Winning Foundation Grants,* our companion volume to this book, is one of many examples that fall within the definition of being strictly foundation-oriented. By far the most comprehensive and significant information source on foundations is the nonprofit Foundation Center, whose publications and services, including its *Foundation Directory* and *Foundation Grants Index,* are detailed in our *Foundation* book. You can also receive free descriptive literature on the Center's publications and services by writing directly to the Foundation Center, 888 Seventh Avenue, New York, N.Y. 10019.

American Association of Fund-Raising Counsel

The majority of the blue-ribbon fund-raising counseling services are members of the AAFRC, a trade organization.

AAFRC publishes *Giving U.S.A.—Annual Report* ($10), a worthy investment for any grant-seeker who wishes a bird's-eye statistical view of philanthropy trends. Well-designed graphics and charts summarize national donations totals broken down into giver (includes corporate) and recipient categories.

The monthly *Giving U.S.A.—Bulletin* presents late-breaking news. If you subscribe ($30 per year), you receive free copies of the *Giving U.S.A.—Annual Report* and the "Master Calendar," a list of upcoming philanthropic meetings, conferences and seminars. For descriptive literature, write:

American Association of Fund-Raising Counsel, Inc.
500 Fifth Avenue
New York, N.Y. 10036

Annual Register of Grant Support

Geared more for the individual fund-seeker than organizations, the *Register* is a 700+ page, hard-cover directory of nearly
1,500 funding sources, including corporations, foundations, government agencies, and associations. There are four quick reference indexes: "Subject," "Organization and Program,"
"Geographic" and "Personnel." Categories are listed by area of
interest and a bonus for the reader is a short guide for writing
proposals. This volume is the best single national source of
funding for individuals, but it does have a couple of chinks in its
armor. First, although its size would suggest otherwise, the *Register* is far from being comprehensive. Second, because of its popu-
larity, many of the listed sources have been overwhelmed with
funding proposals. Almost all large public and college libraries
shelve the *Register* as a standard reference guide. For your own
copy, mail $52.50 to the publisher:

Marquis Who's Who, Inc.
200 East Ohio Street
Chicago, Ill. 60611

Bibliography of Fund Raising and Philanthropy

The most comprehensive bibliography of books, periodicals
and other printed materials dealing with the philanthropic discipline is the 83-page paperback *Bibliography of Fund Rasising and
Philanthropy*. That volume (published in 1975), along with its
updated supplements, costs $22.50. To order or for descriptive
literature, write:

National Catholic Development Conference, Inc.
119 North Park Avenue
Rockville Center, N.Y. 11570

Brakeley, John Price Jones

Full fund-raising services are offered by this long-established private consulting firm, including program development and management, public relations, and funding-sources research. In addition, Brakeley, John Price Jones publishes periodicals such as the *Philanthropic Digest* as well as annual reports on funding programs in the field of higher education. For information on their services and publications, write:

> Brakeley, John Price Jones, Inc.
> 6 East 43rd Street
> New York, N.Y. 10017

Business and Society Review

For big-picture fund-seekers, we recommend *Business and Society Review* ($34 per year). Most issues carry one or more articles that give valuable perspectives on corporate philanthropic philosophy. This periodical is not recommended for those wishing purely pragmatic grant-seeking tips and insights. For a subscription or descriptive literature, write:

> Business and Society Review
> 210 South Street
> Boston, Mass. 02111

Business Associations and Societies

Rich sources of detailed, categorized data on companies are published in trade-association and other types of directories by organizations such as the National Association of Manufacturers and the U.S. Chamber of Commerce. For the names of thousands of these organizations classified by field, consult the *Encyclopedia of Associations* (see page 135).

Business Committee for the Arts

Corporate fund-seekers from the broad spectrum of the artistic world—from music to dance to theater to film to visual arts—have much to be thankful for in the accomplishments of the Business Committee for the Arts. Since its creation in 1967, BCA has successfully encouraged corporations to contribute more generously to meritorious individuals and organizations, be they painters, full-scale symphony orchestras or cultural centers. While it is against BCA's policy to assist your fund-raising program directly, such as by opening a door for you, it will mail you, gratis, a small, helpful how-to booklet, *Approaching Business for the Support of the Arts.* Also ask for BCA's *Examples of How BCA Companies Supported the Arts.* If you like, BCA will be happy to sit down with your organization for the purpose of giving you general advice on increasing your effectiveness in gaining corporate support, as well as listening to your thoughts so that BCA can more effectively serve its mission. Write:

> Business Committee for the Arts, Inc.
> 1501 Broadway
> New York, N.Y. 10036

Business Directories

Several well-researched directories provide essential facts on both major companies and key personnel. These publications usually carry a huge price tag, but fortunately, most business and large public libraries shelve them.

Poor's Register (as it is popularly known) provides data on 37,-000 companies and 75,000 directors and top executives. Information includes brief biographical sketches. This multi-thousand-page, three-volume set is revised annually and is available only on a lease basis: $198 per year. Write the publisher:

> Standard & Poor's Corporation
> 345 Hudson Street
> New York. N.Y. 10014

In addition to *Poor's Register,* consult the *Directory of Directors* and Dun & Bradstreet's *Million Dollar Directory* for supplemental corporate and biographical information.

The Conference Board

Though this prestigious nonprofit organization exists principally to serve its 4,000 dues-paying members, The Conference Board's statistics-filled *Annual Survey of Corporate Contributions* booklet ($5 to members, $15 to the public) is worth the price to grant-seekers wishing to study year-to-year trends in the corporate philanthropic sector. Mail check to:

> The Conference Board, Inc.
> 845 Third Avenue
> New York, N.Y. 10022

CONVO-NCOP

The Coalition of National Voluntary Organizations (CONVO) and the National Council of Philanthropy (NCOP) have joined forces to serve as an umbrella organization for the voluntary philanthropic industry. Active participants include leaders from nearly all major funding sources (including corporate) as well as institutional recipients. Broad-scoped philanthropic issues are delineated and explored at national conferences. For literature on CONVO-NCOP and the next conference, write:

> CONVO-NCOP
> 1828 L Street, N.W.
> Washington, D.C. 20036

Corporate Fund Raising

Although written for local art councils, this 72-page paperback book gives enough solid advice on soliciting gifts from corporations to make its purchase a must for the well-rounded grant-seeker's library. For a copy of *Corporate Fund Raising,* mail $12.50 to the publisher:

> American Council for the Arts
> 570 Seventh Avenue
> New York, N.Y. 10018

Corporations

The topic of how to obtain information from corporations is found in the "Identify Your Information Sources" section, pages 59–61.

Council for Financial Aid to Education

CFAE is a nonprofit organization that has done much to encourage corporations to give financial aid to higher education. As part of its activities, CFAE publishes an extensive series of books and pamphlets, including *The Casebook* ($12), a directory of aid-to-education programs of some 200 major corporations. For a free copy of CFAE's publication list, write:

> CFAE
> 680 Fifth Avenue
> New York, N.Y. 10019

Council on Economic Priorities

One of the functions of this nonprofit organization is researching and disseminating information on corporate social responsibility. For descriptive literature, write:

> Council on Economic Priorities
> 84 Fifth Avenue
> New York, N.Y. 10011

Developing Skills in Proposal Writing

Within this 339-page oversized paperback book the author, Dr. Mary Hall, presents sufficient professional guidance to live up to the title's promise. Besides instructing the reader how to write a proposal, she gives valuable advice on the preproposal stage. The $10 price tag of *Developing Skills in Proposal Writing* should prove to be a worthy investment for most fund-seekers. To order, write:

> Continuing Education Publications
> 1633 S.W. Park
> Portland, Ore. 97207

Double Your Dollar

In its *Double Your Dollar: Matching Gift Details* publication, the Council for Advancement and Support of Education (CASE) has compiled a reasonably comprehensive list of corporations that will match the contributions of their employees. For information on that publication and the companion *Double Your Dollar* leaflet, write:

> CASE
> One Dupont Circle, N.W.
> Washington, D.C. 20036

Encyclopedia of Associations

Three large volumes comprise this extensive listing of over 13,-000 associations in the United States. Volume 1, *National Organizations of the U.S.* ($80), with the aid of a quick-reference alphabetical and keyword index, offers brief descriptions of the associations. Throughout its nearly 1,500 pages, this volume covers a wide range of interests, including various trade organizations. The second and third volumes enlarge upon the information given in the first: Volume 2, *Geographic & Executive*

Index ($65), lists all the associations by state and city, including the names of executives, addresses, and phone numbers; Volume 3, *New Associations and Projects* ($75), updates the first volume. The encyclopedia is a well-established reference guide—most large public libraries stock it, especially the publication's first volume. The volumes can be ordered directly from the publisher:

Gale Research Company
Book Tower
Detroit, Mich. 48226

Financial Development/Nonprofit Management Program

Adelphi University, in cooperation with the National Center for Development Training, conducts a semester-long educational program for individuals seeking a fund-raising career. Tuition: $1,525. For descriptive literature, write:

Fund Raising Management Program
Adelphi University
Garden City, N.Y. 11530

Foundations, Grants and Fund-Raising, A Selected Bibliography

The UCLA Graduate School of Management has compiled the extensive (as of 1976) 67-page booklet, *Foundations, Grants & Fund-Raising, A Selected Bibliography.* For a copy, mail $5 to:

UCLA Graduate School of Management
Los Angeles, Calif. 90024

Fortune 500 List

Each year in mid-spring, *Fortune* magazine publishes a table of the 500 largest industrials, listed in order of sales. A collection of other details is also presented, including the ranking and dollar totals (and comparative percentage) of each firm's assets, net income, stockholder equity, and employee count. A month or two later, the list grows into the *Fortune* 1,000, as the 501st through 1,000th largest industrials are appended. One month later, the *Fortune* 1,300 list emerges, as the "50 largest" are added from six nonindustrial categories: commercial banking, diversified finance, retailing, transportation, utilities, and life insurance.

For us to reprint the names of these firms according to sales or another ranking would be both academic and space-wasting, since the list starts to be educative only when you have the complete data published by *Fortune* magazine. Moreover, while the *Fortune*-compiled data tells you where the corporate headquarters are located, it does not reveal where and to what extent the corporation conducts its business outside its home city—vital bits of information. If you do not subscribe to *Fortune,* or do not purchase the three monthly issues that the rankings appear in, you can obtain a reprint of the most recent listing by mailing $6 to:

> *Fortune* Magazine
> 1271 Avenue of the Americas
> New York, N.Y. 10020

Foundation Center

See the entry "About Strictly Foundation-Oriented Sources," page 129.

Fund Raising Institute

One of this organization's several publications is *Capitol Ideas* ($48), a 320-page, spiral-bound notebook that explains in a how-to fashion the ins and outs of initiating and carrying out a fund-raising program. The *FRI Monthly Portfolio* ($38 per year) points out recent noteworthy fund-raising campaigns and offers helpful advice and insights. For a list of publications and descriptive literature, write:

Fund Raising Institute
Box 365
Ambler, Pa. 19002

Fund Raising Management

Although this glossy, ad-packed, bimonthly trade journal carries few gutsy how-to articles for the specific needs of the corporate grant-seeker, *Fund Raising Management* ($12 per year) does keep you abreast of the innovations taking place in the philanthropic world in general.

Hoke Communications also puts out the *FRM Weekly* newsletter ($52 per year). Write the publisher:

Hoke Communications, Inc.
224 Seventh Avenue
Garden City, N.Y. 11530

The Funding Process

In 120 pages, the authors succinctly guide the reader through the funding maze, from the preproposal to postproposal stages. *The Funding Process* ($6.95 hardcover) can be obtained from the publisher:

Community Collaborators
P.O. Box 5429
Charlottesville, Va. 22903

Funding References

A bibliography and brief descriptions of fund-raising books are contained in 12 offset pages. For *Funding References,* mail fifty cents to:

National Center for Voluntary Action
1214 Sixteenth Street, N.W.
Washington, D.C. 20036

Georgetown University Seminar

"Developing Skills in Proposal Writing" is the title of a three-day seminar offered by Georgetown University. Tuition: $285. For literature, write:

> Continuing Management Education
> Georgetown University
> Washington, D.C. 20057

Getting a Grant

The subtitle "How to Write Successful Grant Proposals" better describes the scope and contents of this 160-page paperback book. For a copy of *Getting A Grant,* mail $4.95 to the publisher:

> Prentice-Hall, Inc.
> Englewood Cliffs, N.J. 07632

Getting Your Share

The Women's Action Alliance publishes a pocket-sized 36-page booklet summarizing the grant-seeking steps including proposal writing. Send $2 for *Getting Your Share* to:

> The Women's Action Alliance, Inc.
> 370 Lexington Avenue
> New York, N.Y. 10017

Grants

Grants: How to Find Out About Them and What to Do Next should be on every grant-seeker's shelf. In her 354-page hardcover work, Virginia White gives invaluable insights and facts on how and how not to obtain grants from corporate, foundation, and government sources. Among the topics covered in this comprehensive book are identifying funding sources and proposal writing. Cost: $19.50. Write the publisher:

> Plenum Publishing Corporation
> 227 West 17th Street
> New York, N.Y. 10011

Grant Seekers

Only the first 68 pages of this 194-page hardcover book deal with the how-to's of grant-seekers. The remainder of *Grant Seekers,* a $15 volume, is devoted to "A Brief History of Major Foundations." Write the publisher:

> Oceana Publications, Inc.
> Dobbs Ferry, N.Y. 10522

Grants and Awards Available to American Writers

For a copy of this 78-page paperback, mail $2.25 to the publisher:

> PEN American Center
> 47 Fifth Avenue
> New York, N.Y. 10003

Grants Magazine

If one would have to select the most sophisticated journal in the fund-raising field, *Grants Magazine* would win the honor. Its broad selection of well-written articles is aimed at both the donor and recipient, thus giving each role a better perspective. Topics range from editorial evaluation of key philanthropic issues to down-to-earth advice on the ins and outs of getting grants from corporations and other sources. *Grants Magazine* is written with fairness and intellectual integrity, two admirable qualities for any publication striving for objectivity. The annual (four issues) subscription rate is $22.50 per year for individuals and $45 per year for institutions. Write:

> Plenum Publishing Corporation
> 227 West 17th Street
> New York, N.Y. 10011

Grantsmanship

For a copy of the 119-page *Grantsmanship* how-to paperback book, mail $4.95 to the publisher:

> Sage Publications
> 275 South Beverly Drive
> Beverly Hills, California 90212

Grantsmanship Center News

One of the most influential media in the fund-raising field is *Grantsmanship Center News*. In the past, some of its articles as well as its reviews on competing publications and services have lacked objectivity. However, most of the *News* content is extremely pragmatic and useful, making a subscription to this bimonthly publication a must for most grant-seekers. The subscription rate is $15 for one, $27 for two, and $38 for three years.

The Grantsmanship Center also conducts fund-raising seminars across the nation, charging nonprofit organizations $325 per enrollee.

For a subscription to the *News* or for the Center's descriptive literature, write:

> The Grantsmanship Center
> 1031 South Grand Avenue
> Los Angeles, Calif. 90015

Grants Register

This 798-page hardcover publication lists scholarships and awards (including those from corporations) available to the individual seeking funding in areas such as graduate work, professional training, or research. The information in the *Grants Register*, including eligibility requirements, addresses, and application procedures, is cross-indexed, providing ease-of-access to awards of regional, national, and international character. Most large public libraries have a copy. For your own copy ($26.50) or for further information, write the publisher:

> St. Martin's Press
> 175 Fifth Avenue
> New York, N.Y. 10010

Guide to Corporate Giving in the Arts

A wealth of source information for people in the art world (broadly defined) is contained within the 402 pages of this over-sized paperback. It gives you facts on the philanthropic activities of over 300 large corporations, under the classifications "For What," "How Much," "Where," and "Why." For a copy of *A Guide to Corporate Giving in the Arts* ($12.50) or for descriptive literature on that and other ACA publications, write:

> American Council for the Arts
> 570 Seventh Avenue
> New York, N.Y. 10018

Guide to Fundraising and Proposal Writing

For $2, you can add to your library a copy of this 42-page stapled booklet, *A Guide to Fundraising & Proposal Writing,* designed for the neophyte grant-seekers. Write the publisher:

> Independent Community Consultants, Inc.
> P.O. Box 141
> Hampton, Ark. 71744

How to Find Information about Companies

If you want a reasonably comprehensive listing of the research sources (government, information services, etc.) on corporations, then this 284-page oversized paperback may be for you. For a copy ($45) or descriptive literature, write the publisher:

> Washington Researchers
> 918 Sixteenth Street, N.W.
> Washington, D.C. 20006

How to Prepare a Research Proposal

David R. Krathwohl's 112-page paperback is a splendid instructional vehicle on how to prepare a research proposal, which happens to be the aptly named title of this book. For a copy, send $2.95 to:

> Syracuse University Bookstore
> 303 University Place
> Syracuse, N.Y. 13210

Lawson Associates

The private consulting firm of Douglas M. Lawson Associates offers a number of services, including general counseling, two-day workshops, and a cassette home-study course. Foundation Research Service, a Lawson subsidiary, publishes *Foundation 500* ($34.50), which allows the grant-seeker to see at a glance the types as well as the geographical distribution of grants made by the nation's top 500 (including company-sponsored) foundations. FRS also publishes Data Files on the top 500 foundations with facts and briefs on foundation personnel and recent grants (cost: $6 per foundation). Write:

> Douglas M. Lawson Associates, Inc.
> 39 East 51st Street
> New York, N.Y. 10022

Leisure Information Service

The biweekly newsletter *Fund Development & Technical Assistance Report* provides information and analysis for funding programs in the leisure-activity field that are offered by both private and public organizations. An annual subscription is $65. Write the publisher:

> Leisure Information Service
> 729 Delaware Avenue, S.W.
> Washington, D.C. 20024

Libraries

Your local public library is an excellent source for obtaining information on corporations—ask the reference librarian. Also, ask permission to peruse the shelves of other athenaeums, such as those small, specialized private business libraries found in some communities. College libraries are another data fount. Of particular interest to you are the higher-education institutions that spring up all over the country: graduate business schools, each of which maintains a business-oriented library containing particulars on many local corporations.

Marts & Lundy

Services of this long-established fund-raising consulting firm range from full campaign management to long-term development strategies to public relations. For information, write:

> Marts & Lundy, Inc.
> 521 Fifth Avenue
> New York, N.Y. 10017

Midwest Academy

One of the workshops conducted by the Midwest Academy is entitled "Fundraising for Social Change Organizations." This four-day long seminar runs $300 and covers the gamut of fund-raising, touching somewhat on corporate contributions. Of particular interest to corporate money-seekers is the 100-page oversized paperback book that they distribute, *Open the Books: How to Research a Corporation* ($4.50). For details, write:

> Midwest Academy
> 600 West Fullerton Avenue
> Chicago, Ill. 60614

Money Grubber

Four dollars will get you a copy of *Money Grubber*, a 94-page instructional booklet on fund raising with an emphasis on grant-seeking. Much of the guide's content comprises abstracts of previously published material in the fund-raising field. Write:

> Contact, Inc.
> P.O. Box 81826
> Lincoln, Neb. 68501.

NAEIR

The acronym NAEIR stands for the National Association for the Exchange of Industrial Resources, a Midwest-based non-profit organization that serves as a switchboard between institutions, such as schools, that need equipment and corporations that have surplus equipment to give away. For an annual membership fee of $180, the institution earns the right to submit a "wish" list of a sweeping range of items they need, from paperclips to computers. NAEIR then tries to match up those wants with available corporate surplus. When NAEIR uncovers a cache of goods in excess of written requests, it notifies its members through special bulletins. For descriptive literature, write:

> NAEIR
> 540 Frontage Road
> Northfield, Ill. 60093

National Fund Raising Conference

Virtually all phases of fund-raising (including some relevant to corporate grant-seeking) are covered in this annual three-day conference. For descriptive literature, write:

> National Fund Raising Conference
> University of Chicago Center for
> Continuing Education
> 1307 East 60th Street
> Chicago, Ill. 60637

New Corporate Philanthropy

Want to see corporate giving from the funding executive's side of the fence? Frank Koch's excellent 310-page hardcover book, *The New Corporate Philanthropy,* covers, among other subjects, how some corporate donors evaluate (or should evaluate) the programs they fund. Cost: $18.50. Write the publisher:

> Plenum Publishing Corporation
> 227 West 17th Street
> New York, N.Y. 10011

New School for Social Research

This famous pace-setting school offers an evening program leading to a master's degree in fund-raising management. For descriptive literature, write:

> Admissions Office
> Graduate School of Management and
> Urban Professions
> New School for Social Research
> 66 Fifth Avenue
> New York, N.Y. 10011

Newspapers and Magazines

Your local newspaper's business section carries articles and announcements of such business events as the opening of a new plant or the promotion of an executive, facts that can be useful to corporate fund-raisers. Worthy business periodicals with a national perspective include *Fortune, Business Week, Forbes,* and *The Wall Street Journal.* Consult your local library's most recent edition of the *Reader's Guide to Periodical Literature* for possible corporate philanthropic stories published in the general interest magazines. Specialized reader's guides will help you find relevant material in the special-interest periodicals.

New York University Seminars

Through its School of Continuing Education, New York University conducts two-day fund-raising seminars in both Washington, D.C., and New York City. The cost of the seminar is $295 per individual for tuition plus a $75 organization-registration fee. Descriptive information is available by writing to:

NYU Conference Center
360 Lexington Avenue
New York, N.Y. 10017

Oryx Press

The world of academia is the target audience for the services of Oryx Press. Private and public grants in nearly 100 academic areas are described in the *Grant Information System,* which is supplemented by monthly *Faculty Alert Bulletins* in six areas: "Creative & Performing Arts," "Education," "Health," "Humanities," "Physical & Life Sciences," and "Social Sciences." Cost: $375 per year. Other Oryx Press works include the annual *Directory of Research Grants* ($37.50), which provides details on over 2,000 grants, the monthly *ELHI Funding Sources Newsletter* ($75 per year) geared for the elementary and high school sector,

and the monthly *Fund Sources in Health and Allied Fields* Newsletter ($95 per year). For descriptive literature, write:

> Oryx Press
> 3930 East Camelback Road
> Phoenix, Ariz. 85018

Philanthropy and the Business Corporation

One of the classic books on the world of corporate philanthropy is Marion R. Fremont-Smith's *Philanthropy and the Business Corporation.* While her book does not give how-to tips for
grant-seekers, it does provide them with valuable insight into
corporate giving from the business executive's perspective. For a
copy of the 110-page paperback, mail $3.95 to the publisher:

> Russell Sage Foundation
> 230 Park Avenue
> New York, N.Y. 10017

Preparing and Writing Proposals

Bryant College offers a one-day (with a free optional follow-up
day) proposal-writing workshop for $85. For literature, write:

> Center for Management Development
> Bryant College
> Smithfield, R.I. 02917

Professional Consulting Firms

Pervading the fund-raising industry are dozens of consulting
organizations whose services as well as fees vary considerably.
You will find brief descriptions of nearly all the more prominent
firms in their proper alphabetical sequence elsewhere in Part
Four. As supplemental material, you may wish to request from

the American Association of Fund-Raising Counsel (500 Fifth Avenue, New York, N.Y. 10036) a free copy of its *Directory of Members* booklet.

The principal users of the services of a fund-raising consulting firm are the grant-seekers short on time, expertise, and/or desire for the drudgery associated with research, but with sufficient money to pay the fees and expenses. A medium-sized college, therefore, is more likely to avail itself of the services than is a giant university such as Harvard, which has a large, sophisticated, well-financed development office staffed with full-time professionals, or, in contrast, a minuscule school such as Boondock College that has a skimpy fund-raising budget with staff to match.

Do not be misled by the bragging of some grant-seeking professionals who claim they raised so many millions of dollars. Such figures are easy to create out of a vacuum, and even if the numbers are true, the credit for winning the grant often belongs to the institution's fine reputation, its golden contacts, and/or the project's undeniable need and quality rather than to the braggadocio's doings. What impresses us the most is someone who obtains a grant for a nonestablished organization.

While the world of professional fund-raising firms has less than a pristine image in the eyes of many grant-seekers, most of these organizations do not deserve that ignominy because—in the right circumstances—they do increase the cost-efficiency of soliciting money. If you have raised, say, $500,000, a $5,000 or even $25,000 fee is not unreasonable.

The secret of prosperously using these firms is to investigate them thoroughly, to ascertain exactly what you are purchasing and whether it meets your needs and budget, and to use their services judiciously. Our experience has shown that too many nonprofit organizations buy a pig in a poke.

Public Management Institute

Two oversized loose-leaf books are published by PMI: *The Grant Writer's Handbook* and *The Grants Planner* ($39.50 each).

Both of these how-to books have well-designed self-teaching formats that facilitate the learning process. To order or for descriptive literature, write the publisher:

> Public Management Institute
> 333 Hayes Street
> San Francisco, Calif. 94102

Public Service Materials Center

The private PSMC organization markets a broad selection of how-to books on fund raising. For its descriptive literature, write:

> Public Service Materials Center
> 355 Lexington Avenue
> New York, N.Y. 10017

Putting the Fun in Fund Raising

This 177-page hardcover book describes hundreds of fundraising events, some of which are potential magnets for corporate funds. For a copy of *Putting the Fun in Fund Raising,* mail $10.95 to:

> Contemporary Books, Inc.
> 180 North Michigan Avenue
> Chicago, Ill. 60601

The Rich Get Richer and the Poor Write Proposals

"Lively" describes the style and format of the 147-page, oversized paperback titled *The Rich Get Richer and the Poor Write Proposals* ($5.50). It covers corporate, foundation, and governmental grant-seeking from the research through proposal-writing stages. For the book or literature, write:

Citizen Involvement Training Project
University of Massachusetts
Amherst, Mass. 01003

Social Register

In the *Social Register* series you will find career and personal information on prominent social leaders of 13 metropolitan areas: New York, Washington, Philadelphia, Chicago, Boston, St. Louis, Pittsburgh, Cleveland, Cincinnati, Dayton, San Francisco, Baltimore, and Buffalo.

Included in each entry are the individual's address, educational background, and social and professional affiliations. Most large public libraries will have the local directory. To order your own local copy, or for further information, write the publisher:

Social Register Association
381 Park Avenue South
New York, N.Y. 10016

Special Events

Some special events can draw corporate support. Two worthy how-to books on the subject are the 220-page paperback *Grass Roots Fundraising Book* ($4.95; The Youth Project, 1000 Wisconsin Avenue, Washington, D.C. 20007) and the 224-page hardcover *Handbook of Special Events for Nonprofit Organizations* ($12.95; Follett Publishing Company, 1010 West Washington Boulevard, Chicago, Ill. 60607). If applicable to your needs, also consider purchasing the 160-page paperback *Presenting Performances* ($2.95; New England Foundation for the Arts, 8 Francis Avenue, Cambridge, Mass. 02138).

Think twice before throwing away a program for an event such as a ballet or gala ball if it contains the names of corporations that have contributed money or the goodwill advertisements that corporations sponsor. The more your project resembles the event in question, the more golden are these play-bills and souvenir programs.

Taft & McKibbon

One of the most sophisticated private fund-raising counseling firms for nonprofit organizations is Taft & McKibbon. Two of its reference books are *Corporate Foundation Directory* (details on hundreds of company-sponsored foundations) and *Trustees of Wealth* (bibliographical data on foundation officers). They cost, respectively, $95 and $90 each.

The organization also publishes monthly *News Monitor of Philanthropy* and its insert, the *Taft Reporter* ($45 per year). Taft & McKibbon's paperback book *Swipe File* ($9.95) contains sample proposals.

For literature on Taft & McKibbon's services and publications, write:

> Taft & McKibbon
> 1000 Vermont Avenue, N.W.
> Washington, D.C. 20005

Telephone Directory

Let your fingers walk through the yellow pages of the business volume or section of your local telephone directory. These pages are a quick source for the names, addresses, and telephone numbers of firms listed according to field of interest—Ma Bell has already done the classifying chore for you.

Many of the nation's largest corporations are headquartered in New York City. If you plan to make a number of calls to that city and wish to curtail the tedious time spent gaining the telephone number through the operator, you can usually get a free copy of the current Manhattan telephone directory (as well as the directories for most other large- and medium-sized cities) simply by requesting one through your local telephone business office. Allow several weeks for delivery.

Third Sector News

Published semimonthly, this newsletter gives advance notice of governmental actions and plans that may affect fund-raising strategy. *Third Sector News* costs $97 per year. Write the publisher:

> DM Publishing Company, Inc.
> 1235 Kennilworth Avenue, N.E.
> Washington, D.C. 20019

Volunteer Urban Consulting Group

The VUCG is a Greater New York–based agency that helps link nonprofit organizations or minority entrepreneurs with professional corporate managers who are willing and able to donate their services. For descriptive literature, write:

> VUCG
> 300 East 42nd Street
> New York, N.Y. 10017

Washington International Arts Letter

Members of the cultural arts world should become acquainted with the various publications of the commercial WIAL organization. Its 221-page *National Directory of Arts Support by Business Organizations* ($65) reveals programs and funding areas of over 700 corporations. The world of corporate foundations is covered in another book: *National Directory of Arts Support by Private Foundations* ($55). The firm's flagship publication is its ten-times-a-year *Washington International Arts Letter* ($38 annual subscription).

To obtain descriptive literature or to order the publications, write:

> WIAL
> P.O. Box 9005
> Washington, D.C. 20003

What Direction? Corporate Philanthropy

Five dollars buys you this oversized 34-page booklet covering some of the topics discussed during a 1977 conference exploring corporate contribution issues. For a copy of *What Direction? Corporate Philanthropy,* write:

> National Chamber Foundation
> 1615 H Street, N.W.
> Washington, D.C. 20062

Who's Who in America

Now published as two expansive volumes, the famous *Who's Who in America* publication gives you biographical sketches of more than 70,000 men and women, many of whom are corporate executives and directors. These twin editions (*A* to *K* and *L* to *Z*) detail each person's professional position, personal background, education, and political, business, social, and religious affiliations, as well as the individual's home and business addresses. Four other volumes offer regional listings. In addition, there is a *Who's Who in the World* and a *Who's Who in Finance and Industry.* Some or all of these directories can be found in most large public libraries. For current price and title information, write the publisher:

> Marquis Who's Who, Inc.
> 200 East Ohio Street
> Chicago, Ill. 60611

Your Fund-Seeking Competition

Too many grant-seekers avoid sharing fund-raising information with another nonprofit organization if it happens to be seeking money from sources identical to theirs. "If that organization becomes better armed," they argue, "our fund-raising chances will dissipate." This apprehension is self-defeating in the long run, because few grant-seekers can acquire all the vital facts by themselves. A synergistic relationship develops when information is exchanged; for instance, each of you may learn from the other previously unknown project ideas or, perhaps, the idiosyncrasies of a funding source. Moreover, as you become allies, you will probably be beating each other's drums as you wend your separate ways around the community.

Two or more of you may also wish to launch a federated campaign. Not only is it possible for you to reduce fund-raising costs with such a coalition, but the corporation may be more willing to shell out dollars because it will be impressed by your systematic approach to solving problems and because one of its gifts will help more than one organization. Why not lift up the phone now and try to arrange a meeting with your funding competition over a drink or lunch?

Your Trade

Do not overlook the copious fund-raising data that is normally available within one's field, as that information is typically well focused. If you are not already aware of the trade organizations, publications, and services within your field, start accumulating a list by asking your counterparts in other organizations. The best published sources are the *Encyclopedia of Associations* (see page 135), for listings of trade organizations, and the *Standard Periodical Directory* (most libraries stock it), if you want to identify the trade publications.

APPENDICES

APPENDIX A

History and Trends

History

Corporate philanthropy is not new. Deciphered Egyptian hieroglyphics from the days of the Pharoahs indicate that it existed—at least in an elementary form—as early as 5,000 years ago. Ancient documents also divulge that some wealthy Roman businessmen sometimes helped sponsor events in the Roman Circus. Much later, but still half a millenium before our era, came the memorable munificence of the Florentine Medicis.

Early-American business philanthropy was insignificant by today's standards, but it did exist, especially on the local level.

Nineteenth-century business largess began to take on new forms, such as those isolated but real pre-1864 cases in which conscience-ridden plantation owners voluntarily emancipated their slaves. Surely their deeds should be considered, to some measure, business philanthropy, because their plantations—money-making ventures—incurred financial losses.

One of the earliest large-scale forms of corporate philanthropy occurred in the late nineteenth and early twentieth centuries, when certain railroads gave money to the YMCA, which constructed and maintained housing as well as social and recreational facilities that were used by the transient railroad employees.

Coincident with the symbiotic YMCA-railroad relationship

was a change in public attitude: more people began believing that the business community had a responsibility to the general welfare of the populace. During this same period, many of the industrialists whose names are associated with megabuck philanthropy—Carnegie, Ford, Mellon, Rockefeller, among others— were accumulating the wealth that would eventually provide the fuel for leviathan grant-making machines.

Corporate philanthropy, as we know it today, did not come of age until World War I. According to the late distinguished philanthropy scholar F. Emerson Andrews, the watershed years were probably 1917 and 1918, when American business entities donated a then-astounding record total of approximately $50 million per year—principally to the Red Cross, which cleverly persuaded some of the large corporations to declare a "Red Cross dividend." When the war ended, so did the magnitude of the corporate largess.

During the Roaring Twenties, corporate philanthropy was hamstrung by the concern, voiced mainly by corporate lawyers, that it might be illegal for a publicly held firm to make charitable donations. Corporate philanthropy was even more devastatingly crippled when the Great Depression withered if not killed profits. As the nation's economy slowly recovered in the mid and late 1930s, so did business philanthropy, but the total still fell short of the money corporations gave during the bumper fund-raising years of the First World War.

The next milestone was 1935, the year Congress enacted a new Revenue Act that made it officially legal for corporations to donate to charity up to 5 percent of their pretax earnings—and to take a tax-deduction for those gifts. At last the basic issue of the legality of corporate giving was settled. Much of the credit for engineering this piece of legislation into the 1935 Revenue Act belongs to the ancestors of today's United Way.

The year 1936 was another significant year: The Ford Foundation was born of the fruits of the Ford Motor Company empire. Before the foundation was created, Henry Ford and his ill-fated son, Edsel, jointly owned a 96.5 percent of the Ford

Motor Company stock (the remaining 3.5 percent was in the hands of Mrs. Henry Ford). The untimely death of Edsel posed a baffling problem to Henry: how to keep the government from devouring a big portion of the Ford pie in the form of inheritance taxes, thereby forcing the family to sell a hefty chunk of its stock holdings and in the process, to lose some of the control of the company.

The Ford tax attorneys adroitly transferred 88 percent of the company's assets to the nascent Ford Foundation in form of non-voting stock, giving the family a tax-deduction in the process. When Henry Ford died, his and his son's estates still clutched virtually total control of the company and had to face only a relatively small inheritance tax bite, an estimated $30 million. That sum is indeed petite when you consider that the company assets were then valued in the neighborhood of $3 billion. The family also (at that time) had much control over how the foundation's immense funds would be spent.

The year 1936 was notable in yet another way: The dollar value of the total corporate tax-deductible charitable contributions in the United States began to be tallied. The following chart is based on those IRS-compiled figures as well as on data from The Conference Board and the U.S. Department of Commerce, as well as from estimates by the American Association of Fund-Raising Counsel.

Year	CORPORATE PRETAX PROFITS (Millions)	CORPORATE DONATIONS (Millions)	DONATIONS AS A % OF PRETAX PROFITS
1936	$ 7,900	$ 30	0.39%
1937	7,900	33	0.42
1938	4,100	27	0.65
1939	7,200	31	0.43
1940	9,300	38	0.41
1941	17,700	58	0.33
1942	21,500	98	0.46
1943	25,100	159	0.63
1944	24,100	234	0.97
1945	19,700	266	1.35

Year	CORPORATE PRETAX PROFITS (Millions)	CORPORATE DONATIONS (Millions)	DONATIONS AS A % OF PRETAX PROFITS
1946	24,600	214	0.87
1947	31,500	241	0.77
1948	35,200	239	0.68
1949	28,900	223	0.77
1950	42,600	252	0.59
1951	43,900	343	0.78
1952	38,900	399	1.03
1953	40,500	495	1.22
1954	38,100	314	0.82
1955	48,400	415	0.86
1956	48,600	418	0.86
1957	46,900	419	0.89
1958	41,100	395	0.96
1959	51,600	482	0.93
1960	48,500	482	0.99
1961	48,600	512	1.05
1962	53,600	595	1.11
1963	57,700	657	1.14
1964	64,700	729	1.13
1965	75,200	785	1.04
1966	80,700	805	1.00
1967	77,300	830	1.07
1968	85,600	1,005	1.17
1969	83,400	1,055	1.26
1970	71,500	797	1.11
1971	82,000	865	1.05
1972	96,200	1,009	1.05
1973	115,800	1,174	1.01
1974	126,900	1,200	0.95
1975	120,400	1,202	1.00
1976	155,900	1,465(est.)	0.94
1977	173,900	1,700(est.)	0.98
1978	202,600	2,000(est.)	1.01

(Bear in mind that the preceding donation figures do not include charitable contributions that corporations wrote off as standard business expenses, a total that we estimate to be approximately equal to the amounts itemized in the charts.)

As a quick glance at the chart will show, the dollar total of corporate contributions started to expand appreciably at the onset of World War II. That military conflict, as well as the subsequent Korean and Vietnam wars, created an economic boom that helped corporate giving surge to new heights. With the exception of the counter-trend years that nipped the heels of those three Armageddons (respectively, 1946, 1954, 1970), the upward trend has been more or less consistent. However, also note that since 1952, corporate donations as a percentage of corporate pretax profits have fluctuated closely around the 1 percent figure.

Corporations spawned company-sponsored foundations in wholesale lots during the Korean War, principally because of the tax advantage. At that time the corporate tax rate for some firms reached a profit-guzzling 82 percent because of the additional burden of the excess-profits tax. If a corporation had an ongoing policy of donating money to charities, it could save money by transferring a huge pile of funds to its foundation during the high-tax-rate Korean War years. Then it would dole out those reserve assets to charities in the ensuing lower-tax-rate years. As a bonus, the corporation could decide—within legal limitations—how those foundation funds would be spent.

Before 1953 there was no legal precedent for corporations donating to a cause in which they received no direct benefit. That year the New Jersey court, in a landmark decision now referred to as the A. P. Smith case ruled that corporations could do so. This means, for instance, that a snowbound ski resort in Aspen, Col., could make a tax-deductible gift to a tropical-fish research center thousands of miles away in Hawaii.

A corporate-philanthropy watcher had much to observe from the mid 1960s into the 1970s. First, a significant portion of the public slowly but surely shed the notion that corporations had the inalienable right to contribute to causes of their choosing without being accountable to the public. Perhaps even more important, these Americans began to learn that they could stand up to corporations that committed antisocial acts such as polluting the environment. When the corporate world became more conscientious about the high long-term cost of fomenting public hostility, the "corporate social responsibility" concept was readily grasped and put into action—mainly for ulterior motives, if truth be told. One of the gargantuan outgrowths of the corporate social-responsibility movement was the $2 billion poured into the inner-city Urban Investment Program by the insurance industry.

A second salient change witnessed within the last generation was a modification in funding-area emphasis. Even though the dollar totals in the health and welfare categories swelled from $63 million in 1962 to $228 million in 1978, the percent of the aggregate corporate-contribution dollar that went into these categories dropped in that fifteen year period from 40.9 percent to 38.3 percent. Education programs suffered a similar decline, from 41.9 percent to 35.7 percent. In contrast, the statistics for culture and art programs jumped from 5.3 percent to 9.0 percent. The downward swing in percentage for the health, welfare, and education funding areas does not reveal the full story. More companies are contributing to new program areas such as drug rehabilitation, but most statisticians still assign those amounts to the health, welfare, and education categories, and thus changes in program emphasis are not apparent. Another example: Scholarships designed for women typically show up as part of the education total rather than being itemized under a title containing the words *women* or *equal opportunity*.

The Tax Reform Act of 1969 affected more than foundations. It also changed some ground rules on how a firm could write off a charitable donation paid with corporate assets. Before the 1969 legislation, a corporation could deduct the fair market value of a gift-in-kind donation. If a company's product had a remarkably high mark-up, it was possible to make money by giving the goods to charity. Let us take a hypothetical example: a pharmaceutical firm donated $100,000 worth of pills that it produced for $20,000. Assuming that it was in the incremental 50 percent tax bracket, it reduced its taxes by $50,000 by claiming the $100,000 deduction. This ruse yielded it a net gain of $30,000 (the $50,000 tax-saving less than $20,000 manufacturing cost). TRA '69

sealed that loophole. Seven years later another piece of legislation, the Tax Reform Act of 1976, further defined and modified
how corporations could legally deduct a charitable gift.

In between these two tax-reform acts, the privately funded
Commission on Private Philanthropy and Public Needs analyzed
and made recommendations on how philanthropy could better
serve its intended purposes. This 1973-established body, which is
popularly known as the Filer Commission (after its chairman,
John H. Filer) urged the corporate world to increase the percentage of its donations from 1 percent to 2 percent of pretax profits,
specifying 1980 as the target date. Obviously, the goal had slight
influence, as the corporate giving statistic still lingers around the
1 percent figure. It was the Filer Commission, incidentally, that
coined the well-known phrase, "Corporate giving is the last
major underdeveloped frontier of philanthropy."

Trends

Prognosticators tread on thin ice, as predictions must eventually face the cruel test of time. We will accept that risk because
we believe we can give you a better glimpse of what may be in
store for you if you allow us to divine a bit with our crystal ball.
Barring unforeseen cataclysmic upheavals such as a radically
new tax law affecting corporate philanthropy, we feel reasonably
confident about our forecasts.

Corporate contribution dollars in America will continue to increase more or less in step with the economy. Whether the long-
sought-after corporate El Dorado will come into being is another
matter. If grant-seekers want to destroy the invisible magnet that
has been holding donations as a percentage of pretax profits to
roughly 1 percent, then fund raisers must develop more creative
tie-ins (see Key Seven, page 68), as well as convince more corporations that contributions create a more conducive environment within which business executives can conduct their profit-
making enterprises.

More executives will learn that it is good business to supply

grant-seekers the information they require. If this change in attitude occurs too slowly, then the "must-disclose-by-law" legislation that is currently being shuffled around in the corridors of
Capitol Hill may become a reality.

The public, with the urging of corporate-social-responsibility
groups, will continue to increase its demands and expectations
that corporations become more accountable to the American
people.

More corporations will use sophisticated tools to measure the
potential visibility and PR benefits that will accrue to them from
each funding option. More corporations will also measure the
success or failure of funded projects just as they currently do for
the money they spend in their firm's operational areas.

More corporations will try to assign better-qualified people to
administer their contribution programs. They will also further
the training of those employees with such methods as letting
them attend outside seminars designed to improve funding
professionalism.

Decision by committee—and especially by the decentralized
committee—will become more of the norm.

A small but expanding number of corporations will be joining
coalitions of other local grant-makers (including independent
foundations). Their goal will be to share wisdom and experience;
or, their aim will be to create a single, more cost-efficient grant-
making center. Regrettably, such a procedure can, if not
checked, encourage the implementation of hyper-conservative
funding policies as a direct result of having to please a diverse
group of contributors.

Just as corporations frequently contract outside services for
functions such as advertising, accounting, legal, personnel, marketing, governmental relations, and international affairs, they
will start to do the same in the area of philanthropy. Corporate
Contributions, Inc. of Princeton, N.J. is one of the pioneers in
this soon-to-burgeon consulting field.

Funding emphasis will change. Some of today's fashionable
programs will almost certainly be neglected waifs by the end of

this 1980 decade, if not sooner. The public's needs and priorities will change too, and many but not all corporations will intelligently alter their giving patterns in response to those developments. Sorry, we are not so much of a soothsayer to foretell precisely which funding-area stars will rise or fall; but we can suggest that more corporations will look upon nonestablishment causes with a more receptive eye.

Corporations will more often specialize in funding areas that relate to their particular objectives, products, and services. This will be in marked contrast to the past, when many corporations plunged headlong into trying to solve a broad array of social ills rather than zeroing in on those areas where they could maximize the input of their expertise.

Matching-gift programs will increase in number and complexity.

Finally, while there will be more corporate philanthropic dollars available, there will be an even greater increase in competition for those dollars. Moreover, the funding quest of the typical grant-seeker will be more sophisticated. The bottom line is that just to keep pace with your competition, you will still have to continue to develop and refine your expertise. No one said fund raising was an easy profession.

APPENDIX B

Sample Corporate Contributions Policy

Most corporations do not publish for grant-seekers a statement of their general operating policy on contributions. One of the exemplary exceptions is the Equitable Assurance Society, which released to the public the following succinct yet informative document:

Nearly all our business activities have social consequences, and the vitality of our organization is affected by social issues. The Equitable must therefore provide monetary and other assistance to selected programs and organizations working in specific areas of social and public concern.

OBJECTIVES

The objectives of the corporate contributions program are:

1. To assist efforts designed to achieve a whole and wholesome society in which our company can flourish, and our Policy-owners, Agents, and Employees can enjoy a high quality of life.
2. To support undertakings designed to bring all people, in particular women, minorities and the disadvantaged, to full and equal participation in all aspects of our national life.
3. To contribute to private initiatives of a public service nature in areas of priority interest to the Equitable.

4. To motivate Equitable people to public service in constructive ways, and to encourage them to participate voluntarily in programs and organizations of their own choosing.

PRIORITIES

Priority will be given to programs, projects, and organizations in the following areas:

Matching Gifts	Health
Education	Human Resources
Affirmative Action	United Ways

In addition, some support will be provided for civic, public and cultural affairs.

PROCEDURES

All requests for charitable or public service contributions from the Equitable, or situations which may lead to such appeals, should be referred to the Public Service Division of the Corporate Communications Department. Proposals submitted for consideration should include a clear, concise statement of the organization's purposes, a copy of its most recent annual report and financial statements, and a copy of the IRS statement of tax-exempt status.

Our assistance may take any one (or more) of several forms—for example: direct grants, matching gifts, purchase of benefit tickets, loaning Equitable personnel, or the provision of services. The budget for such expenditures is carefully developed, and once approved the authority for implementation rests with the Public Service Division of the Corporate Communications Department, which is the only area authorized to use the contributions account.

APPENDIX C

Student Aid

The subject of financial aid to students is beyond the scope of this book. Nevertheless, most students should find some worthwhile general tips and insights on corporate giving in Part One, "Keys to the Corporate Treasury." For the sake of offering a little more help, we would also like to add a few extra bits of information in this appendix.

Most *Fortune* 1,000–type corporations do give financial aid to students. According to a 1977 Conference Board poll, 55 percent of the responding 779 large companies said that they funded scholarships and fellowships. Our informal survey indicates that some corporations give the cash directly to the students, although most prefer to use conduits such as college administrations or the National Merit Scholarship Corporation. Other forms of corporate student-assistance include internships for college and graduate students and the Junior Achievement program for high school students. We have also discovered a growing trend for large corporations to reimburse, in whole or in part, tuition costs to their employees, particularly if their evening-time academic pursuits lead to degrees and/or knowledge that will accelerate their job proficiency. Nothing wrong with, and much right about, that. The payments for the education, of course, are fringe benefits and are duly treated by the corporate accountants as standard business expenses.

By law, corporations cannot deduct a scholarship as a charitable tax deduction if the funds are used, for instance, to entice a student to work eventually for their firms or to encourage a person to extend his or her employment. Neither can those tax-deductible donations be used exclusively for the benefit of the employees or their family members. A minimum percentage of outsiders must be impartially considered for the student financial aid (the formula is too complicated and, especially, too ephemeral to be published here).

For directory-style details, we direct your attention to these two well-established tomes: *Annual Register of Grant Support* and *Grants Register*. Both are discussed in their alphabetical sequence in Part Four, "Information Sources." Also consult the many paperbacks found in college bookstores that itemize some of the student scholarships and advance study awards. Last but not least, visit your college's student-aid office—it is usually your best all-around source for up-to-date facts on financial assistance bubbling up from the local corporate philanthropic springs.

APPENDIX D

Tax Exempt Status

The Internal Revenue Service confers its tax-exempt status only to nonprofit corporations performing certain activities. In very general terms, these activities are:

> Charitable
> Educational
> Religious
> Scientific
> Cultural

How long does it take from the time you apply to the date you receive the IRS Letter of Exemption, the document that officially designates you as a 501 (C) 3 organization? That depends on several variables including your organization's reputation, your lawyer's skill, your field of interest, the IRS backlog, and fate. Two weeks to two years are the extremes.

A qualified lawyer can usually do the job for you for $50 to $500, again depending upon a set of variables. If you want to undertake the task yourself, request the proper application form (IRS Form 1023) and instruction booklet (IRS Publication 557) from your local IRS office or by writing directly to

> Commissioner
> Internal Revenue Bureau
> 1111 Constitution Avenue
> Washington, D.C. 20224

Simultaneously check with your states attorney general's office for any existing or pending regulations that may affect your organization.

For an exceptionally detailed instruction on nonprofit organization tax matters in general, consider purchasing *Tax-Exempt Organizations,* a multivolume loose-leaf service. For free descriptive literature, write the publisher:

> Prentice-Hall, Inc.
> Englewood Cliffs, N.J. 07632

A less-detailed and -costly yet still reasonably thorough primer on forming and administering nonprofit organizations is the oversized 175-page *Nonprofit Arts Organizations* paperback. Though it has a California orientation, the majority of its contents is germane to nonprofit organizations throughout the country. For your copy, mail $12.00 to

> Bay Area Lawyers for the Arts
> 25 Taylor Street
> San Francisco, Calif. 94102

BIBLIOGRAPHY

Annual Register of Grant Support (Marquis Who's Who, Inc., Indianapolis, Ind., 1975, 646 pages).

The Art of Fund Raising by Irving R. Warner (Harper & Row, New York, 1975, 176 pages).

The Art of Winning Foundation Grants by Howard Hillman and Karin Abarbanel (Vanguard Press, New York, 1975, 188 pages).

Better Management of Business Giving by Elliott G. Carr (Hobbs, Dorman, New York, 1966, 114 pages).

Business and the Arts; an Answer to Tomorrow by Arnold Gingrich (Paul S. Eriksson, Inc., New York, 1969, 141 pages).

Business in the Arts '70 edited by Gideon Chagy (Paul S. Eriksson, Inc., 1970, 176 pages).

Capital Ideas by M. Jane Williams (Fund Raising Institute, Plymouth Meeting, Pa., 1975, 3 vols., 1,020 pages).

The Casebook: Aid-To-Education Programs of Leading Business Concerns (Council for Financial Aid to Education, New York, 1978, 232 pages).

Commission on Private Philanthropy, Volumes 1-6 (U.S. Department of the Treasury, Washington, DC, 1977).

The Complete Fund Raising Guide by Howard R. Mirkin (Public Service Materials Center, New York, 1975, 159 pages).

The Conscience of the Corporations; Business and Urban 1967-1970 by Jules Cohn (The Johns Hopkins Press, Baltimore, Maryland, 1971, 122 pages).

Corporate Fund Raising, A Practical Plan of Action by W. Grant Brownrigg (American Council for the Arts, New York, 1978, 72 pages).

Corporate Giving by F. Emerson Andrews (Russell Sage Foundation, New York, 1952, 361 pages).

Corporate Philanthropic Public Service Activities by James F. Harris and Anne Klepper (The Conference Board, New York, 1976, 61 pages).

Corporate Planning for Nonprofit Organizations by James M. Hardy (Association Press, New York, 1972, 117 pages).

Corporate Power and Social Responsibility: A Blueprint for the Future by Neil H. Jacoby (Macmillan Publishing Co., Inc., New York, 1973, 282 pages).

Corporate Responsibility in a Changing Society by Phillip I. Blumberg (Boston University School of Law, 1972, 141 pages).

Corporate Social Responsibility and the Institutional Investor; A Report to the Ford Foundation by Bevis Longstreth and H. David Rosenbloom (Praeger Publishers, New York, 1973, 104 pages).

The Corporation and the Arts by Richard Eells (Macmillan Publishing Co., Inc., New York, 1967, 365 pages).

The Corporation and the Campus edited by Robert H. Connery (Praeger Publishers, New York, 1970, 187 pages).

Corporation Giving in a Free Society by Richard Eells (Harper & Brothers, New York, 1956, 210 pages).

Culture & Company; A Critical Study of an Improbable Alliance by Alvin H. Reiss (Twayne Publishers, Inc., New York, 1972, 309 pages).

Designs for Fund-Raising by Harold J. Seymour (McGraw-Hill Company, New York, 1966, 210 pages).

Developing Skills in Proposal Writing by Mary Hall (Continuing Education Publications, Portland, Ore., 1977, 339 pages).

Dirty Business: the Corporate-Political Money-Power Game by Ovid Demaris (Harper's Magazine Press, New York, 1974, 442 pages).

Do or Die: Survival for Nonprofits by James C. Lee (Taft Products, Inc., Washington, D.C., 1974, 102 pages).

The Funding Process by Virginia A. and Larry E. Decker (Community Collaborators, Charlottesville, Va., 1978, 120 pages).

Fund Raising, A Comprehensive Handbook by Hilary Blume (Routledge & Kegan Paul, Boston, 1977, 188 pages).

Fund Raising, A Professional Guide by William R. Cumerford (Ferguson E. Peters Company, Fort Lauderdale, Fla., 1978, 347 pages).

Fund Raising for Philanthropy by Gerald S. Soroker (Pittsburgh Jewish Publication and Education Foundation, 1974, 190 pages).

Getting a Grant by Robert Lefferts (Prentice-Hall, Inc., Englewood Cliffs, N.J., 1978, 160 pages).

Grants by Virginia P. White (Plenum Press, New York, 1975, 354 pages).

The Grant Seekers by Hal Golden (Oceana Publications, Inc., Dobbs Ferry, N.Y., 1976, 194 pages).

Grants from Soup to Nuts by Sally J. Oleon (Queensborough Community College, New York, 1975, 41 pages).

Grantsmanship by Armaud Lauffer (Sage Publications, Beverly Hills, Calif., 1977, 119 pages).

Grantsmanship Is Never Having to Say You're Broke (National Drug Abuse Center, Arlington, Va., 1975, 39 pages).

Granstmanship: Money And How to Get It (Marquis Who's Who, Inc., Chicago, 1978, 47 pages).

The Grantsmanship Workplan (The Eckman Center, Woodland Hills, Calif., 1977, 103 pages).

The Grant Planner (Public Management Institute, San Francisco, 1979, 256 pages).

The Grant Writer's Handbook (Public Management Institute, San Francisco, 1978, 343 pages).

The Grass Roots Fundraising Book by Joan Flanagan (Swallow Press, Chicago, 1977, 220 pages).

A Guide to Corporate Giving in the Arts (American Council for the Arts, New York, 1978, 402 pages).

Guide to Corporations; a Social Perspective (The Swallow Press, Inc., Chicago, 1974, 393 pages).

Guide to Successful Fund Raising by Bernard P. Taylor (Groupwork Today, Inc., South Plainfield, N.J., 1976, 134 pages).

How to Create a Winning Proposal by Jill Ammon-Wexler and Catherine Carmel (Mercury Communications, Santa Cruz, Calif., 1978).

How to Find Information About Companies (Washington Researchers, Washington, D.C., 1979, 284 pages).

How to Prepare a Research Proposal by David R. Krathwohl (Syracuse University Bookstore, Syracuse, N.Y., 1977, 112 pages).

The Incentive Grant Approach in Higher Education: A 15-year Record by Martin Finkelstein (George Washington University, Washington, D.C., 1976, 56 pages).

The Limits of Corporate Responsibility by Neil W. Chamberlain (Basic Books, Inc., New York, 1973, 236 pages).

Mediability: A Guide for Nonprofits by Len Biegel and Aileen Lubin (Taft Products, Inc., Washington, D.C., 1975, 110 pages).

Minding the Corporate Conscience 1978 (Council on Economic Priorities, New York, 1977, 113 pages).

Money Business (The Artists Foundation, Boston, 1978, 109 pages).

The Money Givers by Joseph C. Goulden (Random House, New York, 1971, 341 pages).

The New Corporate Philanthropy by Frank Koch (Plenum Press, New York, 1979, 305 pages).

The New Patrons of the Arts by Gideon Chagy (Harry N. Abrams, Inc., New York, 1972, 128 pages).

Philanthropy and the Business Corporation by Marion R. Fremont-Smith (Russell Sage Foundation, New York, 1972, 110 pages).

Policies Underlying Corporate Giving by Ralph Lingo Thomas (Prentice-Hall, Inc., Englewood Cliffs, New Jersey, 1966, 127 pages).

Preparing Instructional Objectives by Robert F. Mager (Fearon Publishers, Inc., Belmont, Calif., 1975, 136 pages).

Putting the Fun in Fund Raising: 500 Ways to Raise Money for Charity by Phillip T. Drotning (Contemporary Books, Inc., Chicago, 1979, 177 pages).

The Rich Get Richer and the Poor Write Proposals by Nancy Mitiguy (University of Massachusetts, Amherst, Mass., 1978, 146 pages).

The Social Audit for Management by Clark C. Abt (Amacon, New York, 1977, 278 pages).

Social Responsibility and the Business Predicament edited by James W. McKie (The Brookings Institution, Washington, D.C., 1974, 361 pages).

The State of the Arts and Corporate Support edited by Gideon Chagy (Paul S. Eriksson, Inc., 1971, 184 pages).

Taxation of Charitable Giving by Stephen S. Goldberg (Practicing Law Institute, New York, 1973, 347 pages).

20 Company-sponsored Foundations by John H. Watson III (National Industrial Conference Board, New York, 1970, 84 pages).

Up Your Accountability by Paul Bennett (Taft Products, Inc., Washington, D.C., 1975, 66 pages).

User's Guide to Funding Resources, compiled and edited by Stephen E. Nowlan et al. of Human Resources Network (Chilton Book Company, Radnor, Pa., 1975, 881 pages).